**Community Homes for
the Retarded**

Community Homes for the Retarded

Edited by

Joel S. Bergman
Smith College

with contributions by

Joan C. Cronin
William P. Gerry
Margaret Tomasko Gerry

Lexington Books
D. C. Heath and Company
Lexington, Massachusetts
Toronto   London

Library of Congress Cataloging in Publication Data
Main entry under title:

Community homes for the retarded.

   Bibliography: p.
   Includes index.
   1. Mentally handicapped—Home care—United States. 2. Half-way houses—United States. I. Bergman, Joel S., ed. [DNLM:
1. Community mental health services—United States. 2. Halfway
houses. 3. Mental retardation—Rehabilitation. WM27 AA1 C7]
HV3006.A4C64   362.3   74–15546
ISBN 0–669–96115–9

Published simultaneously in Canada

Printed in the United States of America

International Standard Book Number: 0–669–96115–9

Library of Congress Catalog Card Number: 74–15546

To the fifty people living in
our community homes, and to the
one hundred and eighty thousand
presently institutionalized
people who should have the same
opportunity to live in these
homes.

Contents

List of Tables

Foreword

Deinstitutionalization, the loudly advertised governmental policy of the early 1970s, has fallen far short of its announced goals, and while there are of course differences from state to state, in some localities at least the negative responses both from the community at large and from professional workers seem to outweigh the modest gains achieved in terms of newly established adequate community facilities.

The reasons for this should be obvious: whatever planning may have been undertaken by the central authority on the state level simply was not related to the realities on the community level—such as the lack of experience in establishing community residences, the hiatus between available buildings and the requirements of local codes (necessitating expensive alterations), and the problem of finding and training appropriate residential staff. Other serious obstacles resulted from the inability of a state bureaucracy used to massive institutions to deal with a large number of small community-based residential projects, and from the unavailability of knowledgeable state staff capable of guiding and assisting the local projects.

That there has been any progress at all is mainly due to the wisdom, inventiveness, and commitment of community groups and their staffs, and that is what this book is all about. It allows us to observe at close quarters, step by step, the process of developing group homes in one community. While this might seem to impose certain limitations on the applicability of the material presented, it has allowed for a specificity which is helpful to the reader. So much of our literature is geared to the problems of the larger cities that planners should welcome this firsthand account from a smaller community.

Gunnar Dybwad
Gingold Professor of Human
   Development
Florence Heller Graduate School
Brandeis University

Preface

During the past twenty years there has been a re-evaluation of the purpose and the effectiveness of mental institutions and state schools for the retarded. More and more workers in the helping professions, and the public, are beginning to see that most of these institutions provide at best custodial care and at worst are simply warehouses for human beings. This major change in viewing institutions has been fostered by concurrent changes in values observed in the different domains of our social structure. For example, the community mental health movement has emphasized that human services should be available to people in their own communities rather than extracting people from their communities and requiring them to live in strange places and areas where services are allegedly available.

The communication industry has periodically provided programs, films, and exposés depicting the infrahuman conditions and indignities experienced by institutionalized people. These exposés have been helpful in informing the public about these conditions. Publicizing these conditions has been effective in placing pressure on politicians and bureaucrats to change or to find alternatives to institutions.

The legal rights movement for the poor has been instrumental in showing how much of institutional life is in violation of an individual's civil liberties. Litigation has also demonstrated how state institutions and state officials can be held legally responsible for violating a patient's civil liberties.

What then are the alternatives to institutions? One "alternative" is to discharge formerly institutionalized people into the community without providing the necessary funds for community services for these people. This "solution" has been attempted in California and New York with mental health and state officials still trying to recover from the public protest and general ineffectiveness of this approach to reduce the census at state institutions.

Another "alternative" to institutions is the placement of formerly institutionalized people into private and public nursing homes. Many, but not all, nursing home settings can be seen as not too different from state hospitals or state schools for the retarded. Both nursing homes and state institutions elicit institutionalized behavior in their residents (withdrawal, passivity, dependency), are isolated from community life and are basically human warehouses, with the former specializing in the aged. In both settings one observes lonely people, with few ties to family or friends, having little or nothing to do, and who are simply waiting to die.

Having nursing homes serve as alternatives to state hospitals and state schools is consistent with the "toilet assumption" ethos in our culture. This ethos consists of cleansing or sanitizing the general population from non-

YAVIS (young, attractive, verbal, intelligent, and successful) people, and hiding these individuals by flushing them away from the main stream of life.

Other alternatives to institutions include returning these people to their families, foster family care, hostels, and sheltered apartment dwellings. Group homes, such as community homes and half-way houses, are another alternative to institutions and are the subject of this book, with an emphasis directed towards community homes for the retarded and handicapped.

There has been considerably more literature available on group homes for mental patients (Apte 1966; Raush and Raush 1968), and for law offenders (Keller and Alper 1970) than for retarded individuals. The absence of literature in this area is probably a result of group homes for the retarded being a new concept. Of the 500 or so group homes for the retarded presently operating in the United States, over 75 percent have been operating five years or less, and 46 percent within the past three years (O'Connor and Sitkei 1973). Research literature available on group homes for the retarded consists of surveys based upon questionnaires (O'Connor and Sitkei 1973) or deals with general programmatic concepts (Nirje 1969; Sigelman 1973; Wolfensberger 1972).

This book is an attempt to describe the origin, development, and current status of six community homes for retarded children and adults. Since these community homes and their on-going programs have achieved a considerable degree of success, it is important to demonstrate that community homes are indeed one of several viable alternatives to institutions. Describing the success of these community home programs will hopefully lead to greater federal and state support to develop additional community homes.

Another reason for writing this book is to give sufficient, detailed information about these community homes to interested people and communities who wish to develop their own community homes. It is thought, perhaps naïvely, that there are people in communities who have been thinking about or who would like to start a community home, but who do not know where to begin or how to proceed. This book is intended to be sufficiently specific to assist people inexperienced about community homes to create and maintain an effective community home program.

Another goal in writing this book is to describe a working model of a community home program that may be applied to other populations of formerly institutionalized people. Many of the chapters in this book describe phases in the development of a community home program that could be applicable to populations of people other than the retarded. Some of these chapters are applicable to the development of community home programs for mental patients, disturbed children, juvenile offenders, alcoholics, and the elderly. Several of these chapters would be helpful to people interested in developing respite care homes for children, adolescents, and perhaps, adults. These respite care homes could provide temporary relief to people seeking refuge from some intolerable living situations in their own homes. Currently, the only refuge from these stressful settings available to individuals is jail, mental hospitals, schools for the retarded, or simply running away from home.

The title of this book accurately reflects the nature and scope of the material in this book. However, some clarifications should be made. First, "community homes" is preferred to the term "half-way house" since this book emphasizes the development of a home-like rather than a house-like atmosphere. Inherent in a home-like setting are opportunities to develop social and self-sufficiency skills that are necessary for an individual to eventually live independently in the community. Half-way house is an ambiguous term with uncertainty as to whether the house is a mid-point between going from an institution into the community or a mid-point between living in the community and going into an institution. The community homes described in this book serve as the mid-point for formerly institutionalized people who are being trained to eventually live independently in the community. These homes also provide permanent residences for formerly institutionalized people who choose to remain in these community homes.

The title of this book is more ambiguous when using the term "retarded." With the exception of a few individuals, the residents in the community homes described in this book formerly lived in a state school for the retarded. Upon admission to this school, some of these residents were probably not retarded in an intellectual-deficit sense of the term but could be considered retarded as a consequence of living in such an institution. The use of the term "retarded" in the title and book refers not so much to the common usage meaning intellectual deficit, but more to the retardation in the development of certain skills such as independence, language, and social skills that is a consequence of intellectual deficiency and/or institutionalization.

In 1972, Riverside Industries, Inc., a sheltered vocational workshop for the retarded and physically handicapped, opened the first of the six community homes described in this book. Bill and Margaret Gerry were hired as housemanagers for this home, and the present author served as the behavioral program consultant for this program. The three of us worked closely together, and learned a great deal about community homes and their residents on a trial-and-error basis. The results of some of these learning experiences are shared in this book.

Around a year and a half after the first home was established, Riverside Industries opened three additional homes. Bill Gerry left his job as housemanager and has become the director of the Community Residence Program for the four community homes. Similarly, the present author has become the consultant for behavioral programs for these four homes sponsored by Riverside Industries.

Late in 1972, a community home for retarded children was developed and sponsored by Community Homes for Children, Inc. This home was the first community home for children established in the Commonwealth of Massachusetts. One of the founders of this organization and the two community homes for children that followed, was Joan Cronin who was instrumental in obtaining full funding for these homes. Community Homes for Children, Inc. presently sponsors two community homes. In 1974, Margaret Gerry became the director of these community homes.

The chapters in this book have been written by individuals who have experience and are currently involved in various phases of developing and maintaining a community home program for retarded people. The chapters cover material that is considered important in ensuring successful outcomes for community home programs. Certain dimensions of the community home program are not considered, either because problems have not occurred in these areas, or because the programs are less than three years in existence and more time is needed to discover longer-term problems that may develop.

The author would like to acknowledge the support received from the Sloan Foundation and from Smith College in providing the necessary time and funds to produce this book. The author is also grateful to his parents, Max and Eleanor Bergman, for somewhere along the line teaching him about human dignity and not to accept the "obvious" or conventional "solutions" in helping the "unfortunates" in our society.

J. S. B.

References

Apte, R. Z. 1966. "The Transitional Hostel in the Rehabilitation of the Mentally Ill," in G. McLachlan, *Problems and Progress in Medical Care*. London: Oxford University Press.

Keller, O. J. and B. S. Alper. 1970. *Halfway Houses: Community-Centered Correction and Treatment*. Lexington, Mass.: Lexington Books, D. C. Heath.

Nirje, B. 1969. "The Normalization Principle and Its Human Management Implications," in R. Kugel and W. Wolfensberger, eds., *Changing Patterns in Residential Services for the Mentally Retarded*. Washington, D.C.: President's Committee on Mental Retardation.

O'Connor, G. and E. G. Sitkei. 1973. *The Study of a New Frontier in Community Services: Residential Facilities for Developmentally Disabled*

Persons. Rehabilitation Research and Training Center in Mental Retardation Working Paper No. 72, Eugene, Oregon, University of Oregon, December.

Rausch, J. L. and C. L. Rausch. 1968. *The Halfway House Movement. A Search for Sanity*. New York: Appleton-Century-Crofts.

Sigelman, C. K., ed. 1973. *Group Homes for the Mentally Retarded*. Research and Training Center in Mental Retardation, Monograph No. 1, Lubbock, Texas, Texas Technical University.

Wolfensberger, W. 1972. *The Principle of Normalization in Human Services*. Toronto: National Institute on Mental Retardation.

**Community Homes for
the Retarded**

1

Initial Steps In Creating
A Community Home
Joan C. Cronin

History has shown that large, impersonal institutions for various popula-tions stifle personal growth and create dependency among their residents. The rigid routines established in any institution, necessary for the mainte-nance and care of large numbers of individuals by small numbers of staff, contribute to a loss of self-image and more dependency for those individ-uals. In mental institutions, jails, and even armies, the need for uniformity and strict rules and routines removes the decision-making power from the individual and thereby serves to suppress any individuality and to stifle ambition. An excellent picture of the self-defeating effects of institutionali-zation can be found in Irving Goffman's *Asylums* (1961). Goffman de-scribes institutional life and the encouragement of socially unacceptable behavior in residents by the very structure of the institution.

It is encouraging to read current literature that recognizes the potential of retarded citizens. It is difficult, however, to reverse the thinking of many parents, some professionals, and the public who, for decades, have been convinced that care and protection are the prime considerations when dealing with the retarded.

The Scandinavian countries have demonstrated that retarded citizens can become contributing members of society—self-sufficient and respon-sible. Robert Perske (1973) has described programs in Scandinavia and their success in allowing retarded citizens to assume the risks and responsi-bilities of everyday life. In his treatise, he defines the attitudes among the so-called normal population towards the retarded.

Where many of us worked overtime in past years to find clever ways of build-ing the avoidance of risk into the lives of the mentally retarded, now we should work equally hard to help find the proper amount of normal risk for every retarded person. We have learned; there can be such a thing as human dignity in risk. And there can be a dehumanizing indignity in safety!

This chapter attempts to outline the efforts of one group of parents and advocates who were determined to reverse the wasting and dehumaniz-ing effects of institutionalization upon retarded people.

Establishment of a Nucleus of Interested Citizens

There are probably many successful ways to establish a community home for retarded people, but the methods and explanations presented here en-

1

compass the necessary procedures followed by a small group of citizens in cooperation with the State of Massachusetts in a pioneer effort. Success for this project has required many hours of investigation and public education. It has also been aided by increasing public awareness of the shocking effects of institutional life and the governmental response to citizen pressure for more realistic and dignified rehabilitation programs for the retarded.

When a community home is planned by establishing a new corporation, it is important to enlist the services of a cross-section of community leaders. The board of directors should include a lawyer, well-known and active citizens of the city or town in which the home will be located, some parents of the retarded, and some recognized leaders in the field of mental retardation. Members of local civic groups are a desirable addition to the board as are accountants, businessmen, and tradespeople from the community. Within the community, citizens serving on city councils, zoning boards, and other civic committees are also valuable board members since they can readily supply information on local ordinances and regulations, thereby saving trial-and-error efforts. In this era of greater public concern for those whose lives are touched by mental retardation, support for a community home within the community is available and should be sought.

Incorporation procedures are best handled by a lawyer. While private, non-profit corporations are eligible for state and federal tax-exempt status, the Internal Revenue Service is presently scrutinizing private, non-profit corporations seeking such status. The presence on the board of competent and free legal counsel can facilitate the qualifying process, and since receipt of government funding, both state and federal, precludes payment of taxes, this is a necessary consideration for an organization planning to utilize public funds.

In the present instance, the local Association for Retarded Citizens (ARC) has played an important role in the establishment and maintenance of the home; members of the ARC are constantly involved in legislation, education, and residential services. Thus, many contacts can be maintained inside and outside of the local area through this organization. For example, there are many programs and services outside of the home situation itself that must be located and adapted to provide the individuals in the community home with the programs they need. ARCs can be very helpful in making sure these services are provided. Further, the ARCs can play vital roles as monitors and evaluators of these services.

A varied board is invaluable in establishing community confidence. While there may be some difficulty in obtaining the services of active community leaders, a sufficient number of people free to act on the advice and counsel of interested civil leaders would ensure an effective board. It is important for these people to become knowledgeable with respect to federal, state, and local regulations and funding mechanisms. As evidenced in the present program, much groundwork and on-going decision making must be done by a non-professional board in order for new programs to be established. While this places an added burden on that small segment of the population who usually are already involved in maintaining a position in the community, self-education at the outset and continuing consultation with professionals can ensure the smooth inception of each new program. Participation in such projects is not for the faint-hearted or nine-to-fivers. Constant up-dating of services and the integration of new thinking and up-graded legislation into on-going programs demands a constant, vital board of directors.

Funding

There are many sources of funding for community programs for the retarded at the state and federal level. Federal sources, such as the Bureau of Developmental Disabilities, which is an arm of HEW, provide start-up funds for certain innovative programs for equipment, renovations, and furnishings. Others—Title funds under the Social Security Act, for example—provide operating funds for eligible community programs. These funds are available to establish and maintain community programs provided that certain standards are met. Some states are currently operating quality community programs for the retarded and are able to utilize these funds; others are in the process of up-grading service delivery in order to qualify for such funds. If a state is committed to reducing the population in state institutions in order to qualify for funds to provide quality community services for retarded citizens, then advocates must press for state agencies to begin addressing this up-grading immediately. The philosophy of up-grading services is espoused by all human service professionals and citizens, but in the bureaucratic process, unsophisticated local groups can be discouraged by the seemingly intentional delays and endless red tape necessary to secure government funding. This should not discourage small local groups who can be effective in rallying support for a specific program and in speeding up processes at high levels. This extra effort can involve newspaper publicity, citizen petitions, camping on governmental doorsteps, or lobbying with legislators.

At present, the evidence seems to be in favor of maintaining community homes programs as much as possible on a contractual basis—that is, by using federal and state funding but maintaining autonomy at the local level. At the local level, there is more individual concern with the personal welfare of residents, and direct contact with legislators and governmental officials is much more effective in obtaining financing and refinancing than would be the case if the budgets for community homes were included in massive area or state budgets that are often reduced without legislators being personally aware of specific programs. At the state level, a large proportion of funding is made available through the federal government (as in Social Security funds mentioned above). Thus, much of the effort in obtaining federal monies must be made through state agencies, and local citizens can provide much direction through their lobbying efforts.

Another innovation in funding has been effected with inter-agency cooperation in programming for the retarded. This makes additional funds available through Welfare, Education, Mental Health, and Rehabilitation. While this plan is excellent on the surface, the unique problems inherent within each agency, as well as the age-old problem of official inability to move off the dime can cause a serious slowdown or even halt the momentum of community programming. To ensure the success and continuation of current programming during the transition from single to multi-agency funding the initial funding agency needs to retain the overall responsibility for quality programming until workable inter-agency cooperation is effected. Reciprocal agreements between departments seem to be the most viable solution to serving the retarded in the community and providing the variety of social, educational, and rehabilitative services necessary for personal growth. With transitional accountability defined, the hazard of retarded people falling between the cracks because they do not neatly fit into one program or another is minimized.

Unfortunately, those dedicated to community programs have been placed in the untenable position of vying for monies desperately needed to up-grade the services in institutions. It is obvious that funding agencies cannot continue to practice this either/or attitude. Therefore, it is necessary to examine the needs of all the retarded within a given area—whether in the institution or in the community—and to focus on programming for individual needs and in an atmosphere of progress in order that available monies can be utilized to the best advantage. One can readily see not only the stresses placed upon institutional administrators and community programmers in the face of limited funds but also the need for a proliferation of long-neglected services and programs to overturn the trends of the last fifty years. Close cooperation among all providers and a definition of goals agreeable to all is paramount.

Local funding can be obtained for the down payment on a suitable home. In this connection, enlisting the aid of private organizations and student groups is effective, and even self-initiated fund-raising efforts have good results. It is desirable to raise some initial funds locally: to demonstrate to governmental funding agencies that there is community support for the program; to publicize the project locally; and in the process, to educate the public. Newspaper articles, and personal apearances by active board members at meetings of local civic organizations to outline the program and enlist support are also effective public education methods. Other community organizations, such as the Jaycees, Lions, Kiwanis, Women's Clubs, and so forth, are very receptive to the needs of the retarded and willingly adopt such fund-raising objectives as needed equipment or furnishings that may not be provided in an operating budget.

In some cases, it is necessary for an organization planning a community home to seek short-term loans for the necessary start-up funds. If the system of funding for community programs is on a refund basis (i.e., monthly reimbursement for expenses incurred during that month), it is necessary to have in hand operating expenses for two or three months to allow for application and processing procedures. In this connection, members of the home board should become knowledgeable of application and budgeting procedures and seek out the state employees at the local and state level who can advise them. The reimbursement practice is the most difficult for small organizations with no surplus monies for the initial months. Without adequate reserves, programs can be jeopardized, and there is the danger of the displacement of house residents.

The Social Security Act provides monthly maintenance income for disabled citizens. Supplemental Security Income (SSI) is available in varying monthly amounts according to the disability of the individual. Medical and dental care is automatically included with this income, and once established, it provides stable maintenance in the community home. While this seems to solve the problem of maintenance within the community home, it is not the answer for all levels of disability; a comprehensive, all-encompassing program of rehabilitation of the retarded is not possible at this time with these funds. It remains for human service agencies to maintain a sensitive concern and responsibility for retarded citizens living in the community. Funding for staff within the home and staff within the community to provide services outside of the home must be provided in sufficient amounts to ensure the necessary follow-up and contact with retarded citizens in the community.

Identifying Population and Developing Programs

The level of functioning of individuals who live together in a community home should be as uniform as possible. Although there are always individual differences, the fact that eight or ten people live together, eat together, and socialize together suggests that group activities and functions can be provided more easily if everyone in the home is at approximately the same functional level. Attempts have been made to provide halfway houses for diverse populations from jails, mental institutions, and institutions for the retarded. This has not proven to be advantageous, for people from these various groups have widely differing programmatic needs that can never be met by a single living situation.

There is a desperate need for community living situations for retarded people from institutions, but these needs also exist for those who have never left the community, and these two groups seem to relate well in one community residence. Programming for retarded citizens who have been in institutions is far from satisfactory, and we should not lose sight of this fact in our zeal to provide a viable alternative to institutionalization. If simultaneous programming is not carried out, those who are neglected today are the institutional residents of tomorrow.

As the population in institutions decreases and old hospital practices are abolished, money can be diverted from the institution into the community as residents leave. In some instances, actual staff from the institution, or perhaps staff positions, can be moved to community programs as the institution's population decreases. However, such moves can and have caused some problems within the institution. Some firmly entrenched staff members, preferring the old institutional habits in caring for the retarded, resist change, which, in view of the strength of civil service and unions, can be the cause of knotty problems. However, with good communications between community and institutional administrative staff and with careful re-education of transitional staff, such problems can be alleviated. Care must be exercised in dealing with institutional personnel who may not be educated to the value of community programs or to the potential of institutionalized residents. Large wards, housing up to forty residents, promote dependence and create additional retardation in development. This dependent retardation is mitigated by the intimate atmosphere and personal involvement of individuals in small programs, which is not readily apparent to institutional personnel at the outset. Therefore some education of staff must be undertaken to establish their confidence in not only the community situation but also the community personnel. A close working relationship between ward staff, social workers, and administrative staff and their involvement in all facets of transition must be maintained. This process can be confounded by the involvement of local ARCs and community mental retardation personnel in the placement and follow-up of institutionalized retarded people from their areas. The dividing line between community responsibility and institutional responsibility can be hazy, and much tact and understanding must be exercised on both sides to effect the smooth transition of clients from institution to community programs.

When a community home is in the vanguard stage, problems inherent in phasing down institutions are at their most explosive, and difficulties arise that may not be present as programs prove successful. Parents and guardians are naturally apprehensive about unproven community programs.

There are myriad reasons why retarded people are institutionalized, and understanding and sympathy with the fears of parents is the first consideration in planning programs outside of the institution. Since the institutional staff is in direct contact with parents or guardians of the residents, a group establishing a community home should work with these staff members in the selection process to facilitate easing parental fears and doubts. Parents are potent forces in promoting and maintaining quality programming, and if organized and well-educated in their role as lobbyists, they can be the most effective group within the structure of community programming. Since they owe allegiance to neither the institution nor the community organization, they must be approached with sensitivity, which can be accomplished either by other, more knowledgeable parents or by professionals who have a real understanding of the economic, emotional, and family problems of parents with retarded children. This point should not be regarded lightly, because, when mobilized, parents are the single, most effective group in promoting change and maintaining quality because of their willingness and ability to persevere.

However, there are many who still feel that physical care is the most important service in providing for the retarded. This attitude is reflected in most of the legislation passed for the benefit of the retarded. Even the Social Security Act (SSI) expounds a philosophy that creates a *Catch-22* situation for the retarded and those working with them: retarded citizens are only eligible for SSI benefits as long as they are disabled. However, as soon as they are employable—even for minimal wages—they are disqualified from SSI and lose their eligibility to live in those community homes funded by the federal government where there is supervision and rates are suited to their means. So, we are embarked on a program of teaching the dependent independence skills and thereby placing them in a position to lose financial support that is still necessary, at least for a time. This policy can also serve to stifle any desire to be independent, and the end result could be as great a dependence as that in the institution.

The size of the program to be administered by one group and the number of residents within the home, remain debatable points. A small, community-oriented group, responsible for a limited program, can remain in contact with the problems of individuals when they arise. Local professional people are more willing to offer their services for a specific program that is well-defined and highly visible in the community. A program that is an extension of larger, state-run programs can become enmeshed in state regulations and locked into practices that may not prove successful. Current civil service practices ensuring the longevity of state employees can impede the processes of change and growth that are a necessary part of good programs. Certainly, states should support programs, but the responsibility and direction of these programs should remain local and autonomous so they can be constantly evaluated and revised without the necessity of legislative action.

The number of clients in a given home depends on the disabilities involved. If staff morale is to remain at a high level and if residents in the home are to receive the individual attention necessary for training and rehabilitation, numbers should be small. A home with ten highly functional residents could be successful with the maximum support of services in the community. However, if there is need for extensive rehabilitation and socialization training in the home, six or eight would be the maximum. Literature is available on community programming involving up to twenty residents in each home in a state program consisting of thirty to forty group homes (Bridges 1973). This type of program, while superior to large institutional programs, must be highly organized and inflexible. Any interruption in the funding could jeopardize the lives of many people. Alternately, a small program of one or two houses involving twelve to twenty people in total is far more homelike and individual-oriented.

Budgeting

Budgeting for the maintenance of the home once established can be easily carried out in accordance with the economics of the area in which the home is located. (A sample budget for home with adult residents is appended.) If an organization cannot expect donations of furnishings and the equipment necessary to operate a home, approximately $15,000 will be needed to furnish the home and maintain the staff and residents for two or three months—until all the bureaucratic kinks are ironed out and reimbursement is flowing smoothly.

Professional consultation and medical and dental care are provided to those people who are eligible for SSI benefits. However, governmental financing for consultative services should be obtained to provide these services for those who are not eligible. There is also a great need to work towards the strategic placement of community professional staff to provide the necessary support services for retarded people in transition. These services should include well-staffed rehabilitation or sheltered workshop facilities; adequate adjustment counseling and follow-up services; legal advisors; specialists in any type of physical or emotional problems; and advocacy programs.

Fiscal Responsibility

Due to the current nationwide effort to minimize the number of persons needing to be institutionalized, the board of directors or governing group must keep up with a large body of information concerning changes in SSI and other legislation that may benefit the retarded. The board must also ensure that it practices sound bookkeeping practices with a certified accountant responsible for the proper management of funds. With so many sources of funding and concommitant diverse reporting requirements, this part of the management of the home should receive close attention.

In most programs, it is the practice for residents to pay a predetermined amount from their own earnings or benefits for room and board in the home. The salaries and maintenance of staff in the home are provided through contractual agreement with state agencies. In an ideal budget, specified amounts are allotted for food and supplies. Housemanagers should be expected to limit their spending to these specified amounts. If unforeseen expenditures not otherwise included in the budget do arise, it is the responsibility of the contracting agency to obtain funds outside of the budget. Here again, local civic groups are a logical source of funds for special projects. As programs expand and funding becomes more divided, good clerical help is necessary. The program director and treasurer of the governing body should work closely with the clerical staff to maintain proper records.

Records pertaining to residents and their development should be maintained by housemanagers. These should be kept up to date at all times and should include education programs, social activities, personal growth and development, goals and methods for reaching these goals, medical and dental records, and any other reports unique to the individual. An accounting of client's funds used in the maintenance of the home must be made available to them or their guardians.

Budgeting for the first year for any community home can only be projective. As each home is unique, there are no specific figures available. The staff—working closest to everyday expenditures in the home—should have the best idea of budgeting after the first year of operation. Since the ultimate responsibility of accounting for expenditures rests with the contracting agency, close cooperation between house staff and the fiscal officer should be maintained to ensure that adequate funds are contracted for to maintain the home and its program.

The contracting agency should be in constant communication with the funding agencies through local staff so that the needs of residents can be met as they arise. There is a danger, when initiating change, of creating funding that is inflexible and designed for purposes of austerity and accountability to funding agencies. This is unavoidable when dealing with SSI or rates set for individuals through governmental agencies. However, the budgeting for community homes should be flexible enough to address the on-going needs of each individual client; populations change, and individual needs of clients change.

Refinancing

The local corporation must be assured of a commitment by the state to the permanent maintenance of community homes. In states where community homes are new, permanently allocated monies are not yet a part of the yearly budget of state agencies. This places on the local corporation the burdens of maintaining the quality of the program and of working closely with mental retardation officials and legislators to assure yearly refinancing. With individual SSI benefits, the pressure on the state agency of total financing of the home is lessened, and staff and consultant salaries comprise the major portion of the budget financed with state funds.

Conclusion

In this chapter, steps in the initial planning and realization of a community home have been set forth. Consideration has been confined for the most part to the mechanics of establishing and maintaining the home itself with citizen participation. Little has been said about the primary consideration of the support and rehabilitative services that must be present in the community for the benefit of the residents in the home. A community home cannot be the total answer to the deinstitutionalization process for it is only one aspect of the many services necessary to provide for growth and social consciousness in the retarded. Therefore, it is the responsibility of the local group administering the community home to see to the total needs of each individual within the program and to instruct staff and professionals to do likewise.

References

Bridges, J. E. 1974. *Establishing and Operating Community Living Centers for Mentally Retarded Adults.* Publication of the Marbridge Foundation, Inc., Austin, Texas.

Goffman, E. 1961. *Asylums.* New York: Doubleday.

Perske, R. 1973. *The Dignity of Risk and the Mentally Retarded.* Publication of the National Association for Retarded Citizens, Arlington, Texas.

2

Additional Considerations in Creating Community Homes for Children
Joan C. Cronin

There seems to be widespread planning of community programs for the adult mentally retarded who have been institutionalized for most of their lives. These programs must necessarily include many training programs and peripheral services designed to eliminate behavior patterns engendered and strengthened by long years in an institution. What better time is there then to offer community programs than during childhood—before institutional and bizarre behaviors become firmly entrenched and require elimination?

Children who presently reside in our state institutions are there primarily because there were no services for them or their families to turn to as an alternative to commitment. If these services had been available, we would not be facing the staggering task of rehabilitating people now in institutions and could focus on the problem of providing complete services within the community from birth. However, the problem exists, and children must not be allowed to languish in institutions and then become adults who must be rehabilitated in order to live in a community setting. One encouraging factor about providing community services for children returning from the institution is that children are more flexible; they learn and unlearn faster and more permanently; their behaviors are less firmly entrenched through years of institutional living.

Special Needs Associated with Children

Some retarded children, especially those with Down's Syndrome, have health problems connected with this condition. Frequently, infection of the upper respiratory system will plague these children through adolescence. However, with the use of antibiotics these infections can be minimized. There are also some health problems—parasites and other conditions not found outside—that are endemic to institutions. Other children are subject to epileptic seizures; this can be disturbing to persons without prior knowledge and training in the procedures to be followed. There are specific orthopedic problems that can be present in mentally retarded children. These specific problems as well as the usual medical problems faced by all parents, point to the necessity of having a well-qualified physician who has familiarized himself with each child and who can be available to housemanagers

11

when the need arises. This physician should also be affiliated with a local hospital so that should an emergency arise, the child can be treated immediately.

Good dental care is a prime consideration since institutional dental care often leaves much to be desired (i.e., orthodonture is often required, but not usually provided in the institution). Most medical and dental care within the institution is on a crisis basis.

Speech and language development therapy is necessary on a constant, individualized basis. The patterns of speech development in retarded children vary widely, and these variations coupled with the inadequate speech stimulation in the institutions require competent, professional staff working both at home and in a day program.

Psychological services must be made available to the home and day program staff to facilitate the adjustment of both children and staff. Other consultation should be provided as needed by individual children.

In a community home where the level of functioning of the children is relatively uniform, extra care should be exercised to develop individualized programs suited to the needs of each child. Many public educational policies require the child to fit the program, and this practice should be discouraged.

The SSI (Supplemental Security Income) assistance has been expanded to include disabled children, which thus relieves parents of the financial burden of specialized, expensive programming and therapeutic services. The current payments provide for reasonable room and board, clothing, and pocket money. With added medicaid benefits, which are provided with SSI, the basic human needs are met and the remaining expenses of staffing, consultation, and maintenance should be provided by state and local agencies.

Education

A systematic program of developmental education should be established before the child leaves the institution. Currently, in Massachusetts, new education laws guarantee all children, regardless of their location and disability, evaluation and prescriptive individualized education. It is, however, the responsibility of the local board, through its staff, to make sure that each child is receiving the necessary service.

A community home for retarded children may include those who will be capable of handling a public school program or those who will need the training offered at a developmental day center. In one home, a mixed population of moderately and severely retarded children was attempted. After a few months of operation this mixture was found to be too diverse in planning programs of training and recreation within the home environment; moderately retarded children from the institution need a freer, less structured home atmosphere, while the severely retarded require more individual supervision and concentrated self-help programs.

In some communities, the public school programs for children with special needs are well-developed and well-staffed so that the children who are moving into the community can find programs suited to their needs. School officials should be contacted before the home is opened so that they may review the needs of the children to be placed in the home and be prepared to provide the necessary individualized programs. The community home board should be familiar with the laws governing the education and the fiscal responsibility for this education of children in community homes, as well as any specific limits that may be placed on the child's attending the public school.

Homes established for moderately or mildly handicapped children can be much more flexible. There is an opportunity for the children to make acquaintances and to interact with neighborhood children and gradually attain the social attitudes that can only be acquired in this manner. It is a difficult task for a child who has been institutionalized for most of his life to learn the value of waiting for delayed rewards and the necessity of compromise in order to remain a member of the peer group.

A home that is established for severely or profoundly retarded children should be located near a developmental day care center, and this center should be involved in the evaluation process and be prepared to offer individualized programming. In a home for severely retarded children who are attending developmental day programs, more interaction with house and day center staff must be maintained. Programming in self-help skills must be carried on both in the home and in the day program with the same goals and guidelines jointly set up by both staffs. Some staff members from the community home may be assigned part-time to the center to ensure an integrated program.

Some programs have followed the proposed practice of combining living and day programs within the same facility. This, however, is not community programming; it creates a mini-institution, and such a practice leads to a rapid turnover in staff because there is no relief from the training situation. While the maintenance of a secure, familiar environment with known routines is the best atmosphere for the severely retarded, this can be provided in a reciprocal program between the community home and an outside developmental center. Children who leave the home each day to go to an educational environment suitable for their needs and mingle with children from other homes can develop socially as well as individually. This opportunity cannot be provided in an enclosed environment where they experience no change in personnel, environment, or peers.

Developmental center staff should receive as much support as is necessary to prevent the degeneration of the community home program to one of only physical care and maintenance. Parents who have kept their children at home even though they are severely retarded have found that well-run developmental centers with specialized staff and supportive programs have enabled them to do so.

Parents

As has been stated before, the parents of children in community programs are the single best resource for exerting pressure to obtain quality programming. In the past, however, parents have been less than completely effective in demanding quality programs for their retarded children. The ever-present security of the institution has kept the pressure off the community and weakened concerted efforts for community support services. Communities have only recently begun to shoulder the responsibility for the education of all retarded children. The institution need no longer be the last resort if parents are willing to risk the initial uncertainties that any innovative programs contain. As taxpayers, they can demand education for all children, and in the process can educate those parents who may not be knowledgeable.

Parents are effective in aiding institutional personnel in providing the best atmosphere for their children in the transition from institution to community. It is the responsibility of a local community homes agency or ARC to make sure that parents of children in institutions are fully cognizant of the necessity for total commitment to community services and to involve them in the planning process.

Parents of children residing in community homes can serve as the most critical and faithful monitors of the programs since it is their prerogative to expect and demand the best for their children. Housemanager relations with parents should be open. Parents should be made aware of programming in the community residence that should be extended to home visits, which, in turn, should influence their behavior with their child during the visit. Parents should be encouraged to visit the community home and to take their children to their own homes for visits whenever possible. A parent group that meets regularly with house staff and any other professionals involved with the home will be able to keep up with changes in programming. Meetings with staff of the day programs, parents, and housemanagers should be held regularly.

Additional Staffing

The usual complement of staff for an adult community home is three persons—two housemanagers and one assistant housemanager. Due to the

Parents &
Community
homes

EXERT PRESSURE

fact that children must be supervised at all times when they are in the home and are more dependent on home staff for guidance, a minimum of five staff members is suggested. This number allows for three staff members to be on duty during the hours that children are at home and provides for two days off per week for each staff member. Hiring a married couple to act as housemanagers is necessary from the point of view of providing a type of parental model for the children. There should be no attempt made to fill the role of natural parents, because only confusion and resentment will result when the housemanagers leave. Since there will be some children whose parents are not involved, the housemanagers or director should find an advocate from the community who will assume many aspects of the parental role. This is not an easy task, for a real commitment to a child is demanded.

Additional staffing is also necessary because children leaving the institution are for the most part unaware of the dangers present in a normal household. In self-contained institutional wards with safety windows and all elements of danger removed, there is little opportunity for the children to learn common home safety precautions. Therefore, this training must be carried on after the children enter the home.

Leisure time in the home should involve a balanced program of relaxation, entertainment, and physical exercise. Institutions cannot provide the necessary programs to promote physical development, and children often become obese and have poor muscle tone. This condition is further aggravated by the large amounts of starchy foods in institutional diets. It is, therefore, necessary to train house staff in the purchase and preparation of well-balanced, nutritious meals and to provide a regular program of physical exercise. Recreation equipment for retarded children need not be over-specialized, but it should be appropriate for the level of handicap. Architects are at present designing playgrounds specifically for retarded children; investigating these designs and employing one of these architects would be a worthwhile project.

Legal Responsibilities

One vital concern of parents whose children are considered for transfer from the institution into the community home is the question of continuity of programs. While their children were in the institution, parents could see a progression of care for life. This is not visible in community programs at this time due to the relative scarcity of adolescent programs and support services and to the newness of the concept of community homes in general.

Deinstitutionalization of state school residents leads to the phase-down or phase-out of institutional care for a certain segment of the retarded population, and parents see the old security snatched away and can only hope for the continuation and expansion of previously unattempted community programming on a large-scale basis. This naturally leads to anxiety and a certain reticence on the part of parents to fully endorse the movement of their children into the community. This also leads to certain legal problems that up to now have not had to be faced by parents. Questions now being raised by parents include:

If I place my child in a community program run by a private agency, what responsibility remains with the state department of mental retardation?

Unless I take legal steps, who is the official guardian of my child in a community program?

Unless lifetime programs are established to provide a continuity of programming under the direction of one responsible, accountable agency, how can I be assured that my retarded child will not be out on the street at some point after I am gone?

As is usually the case during transition periods, all of these questions have not yet been answered to the satisfaction of parents. Small wonder that parents are hesitant about removing their children from institutions.

The question of competency continually looms large. If a retarded person reaches the age of eighteen, he is automatically deemed competent to manage his own affairs unless a legal guardian is appointed through the courts. In the case of a retarded citizen with borderline, or mixed capabilities, who will be the decision-making body to certify him competent or incompetent? This is a question that must be addressed on a state and national basis. Are I.Q. scores or psychiatric evaluations going to continue to be the criterion by which a person is judged competent? Should a parent be named guardian of his own child?

Even in the past, this question has been skirted more often than faced. Certain children and adults in institutions have been admitted via the courts, and a guardian has been appointed, usually by the superintendent of the state institution. Others, however, have been committed by their parents and have reached and passed the age of eighteen with no thought being given to this problem.

Another legal question concerns the responsibility of house staff and others providing care or programming for a retarded child. At present the practice of obtaining parental consent in the form of a signed release relieving caretakers of all responsibility has been found to be useless in the courts. Those hired to provide services for the retarded should be held reasonably responsible when children are under their care. This is a moot question when one considers that indeed the retarded must be educated to take a certain amount of risk (Perske 1973) in order to be considered a part of the general population.

The above questions are constantly being addressed by the legal profession, legislators, service providers, and parents; hopefully answers will be forthcoming. However, it is the responsibility of the general public and especially those concerned with the future of retarded citizens to acquaint themselves with all the problems and then find means to deal with them systematically.

There is, of course, the primary legal question of just how responsible is a governmental agency charged with the education and welfare of retarded citizens. When it delegates its responsibility to private corporations and even in some cases to individuals, just how much responsibility remains within the purview of the state agency? Does it then assume the monitoring and evaluative role that is the responsibility and duty of parents and ARCs? Indeed it has been demonstrated during the last four or five years that small dedicated organizations can provide a much more individualized, quality program than can a bureaucracy that has long since become out of touch with everyday human needs and problems.

Transition from Institution to Community Living

The behaviors induced and maintained by children living in institutions are entirely inappropriate in the outside world. Indeed, this is one of the prime reasons why the general public fears the proliferation of community programs. They don't want those "funny looking and acting people around." The old taboos that originally surrounded the retarded and linked them with the emotionally disturbed and even with witches and demons still live in the hearts of the uninformed. These fears are borne out sometimes by the seemingly bizarre and unexplainable actions and reactions of retarded people who leave the institution. An interesting survey was made of retarded adolescents in institutions in the book *Hansels and Gretels*. Braginsky and Braginsky (1973) found that residents in institutions for the retarded were practicing Machiavellian techniques with ward staff and other professional personnel and, further, that they were fully aware of the games necessary to obtain favors or to survive in the institutional setting. Small wonder that these behaviors are seen as threatening out in the world.

Sex is another controversial question as far as the retarded are concerned. Until recently, sex was completely banished from consideration with the strict segregation of males and females in the institution. There were certainly many incidents that demonstrated that indeed the retarded were of both sexes as was the rest of the population, but these incidents were "handled" and no mention was made of them. Fortunately, now that sexuality is a subject for general discussion, even the retarded are beginning to be recognized as sexual beings. However, adult residents are still being segregated in the community, and there continue to be homes only for men and only for women. As in any other educational process, time and gentle persuasion via example is needed.

All the above points up the necessity of establishing homes for retarded children that include both boys and girls. Families are comprised of both males and females, and it is natural to consider a home with both male and female retarded children. As these children mature and move into adult programs, the natural, healthy acceptance of both sexes can be carried over with them. Thus, programs for children that include sex education in a progressive manner in the home environment will later decrease the need for the elaborate sex education programs for the adult retarded that are necessary at this point because of the effects of institutionalization and segregation of sexes in institutions.

In general, planning a home for children is no more difficult than planning one for adults, as far as the house itself is concerned. There are some added features that are necessary for severely retarded children, but for the mildly and moderately retarded, the closer the home is to normal, the more quickly the children will adapt to community life. Homes for severely retarded children require more safety features than those found in a normal home (e.g., gates across stairs and entrances to danger areas like kitchens; fenced-in outside play areas). However, it was found that plexiglass windows and elaborate alarm devices on bedroom doors to alert the house staff when children leave their rooms at night were unnecessary. These added features may prove a necessity for hyper-active or disturbed children who act out in aggressive or destructive ways, but we have found that ordinary precautions consistently maintained are sufficient for preserving the safety and happiness of the moderately as well as the more severely retarded child.

Staff enthusiasm, affection, and programming skills contribute most to the success of a home for retarded children. If these factors are present, it is almost inevitable that the children will prosper, the fears of parents will be allayed, and the value of such a venture will be proven.

References

Braginsky, D. D. and M. B. Braginsky. 1971. *Hansels and Gretels.* New York: Holt Rinehart & Winston.

Perski, R. 1973. *The Dignity of Risk and the Mentally Retarded.* Publication of the National Association for Retarded Citizens, Arlington, Texas.

3

Selection of Homes
William P. Gerry

The selection of a house is one of the most important decisions to be made when planning a community residence program, and an incredibly large number of factors become involved in the selection process. These include financing, zoning, location, furnishings, and so forth. An incredible amount of planning also enters into the orderly commencement of a program. The following discussion will shed some light on most of the factors to be considered and will supply some information about timing and planning.

The variables involved in this chapter provide infinite possibilities on which the decision may be based, and since the perfect house has yet to be found, a group seeking a community home may be faced with difficult decisions in weighing the alternatives. It is essential to find out as much as possible about a house before making a legal commitment to it, and to aid in the orderly integration of facts concerning a suitable house, a checklist is provided in Appendix C. This form, when completed, can be used to evaluate information about a single house or for comparing data on several houses.

Physical and Spatial Considerations

The general size of the house is a good place to start. The most appropriate number of people in a residence seems to be eight to ten. To go beyond this number places strains on both staff and programming to a great extent and, from our experience, seems to interfere in developing a sense of "group." However, finances may dictate a larger number of residents.

A goal of only single and double bedrooms requires a minimum of five. A kitchen, dining room, recreation room, and a living room add up to nine rooms. Housemanagers should have at least two rooms to themselves, with a private bath and, if possible, a kitchenette. A live-in assistant's room brings the total to a minimum of twelve rooms. If at all possible, two bathrooms should be available for the residents and one for the housemanagers. Twelve rooms, plus two or three baths, should thus be considered a minimum number of rooms for a prospective community home. A larger number of residents in a house adds to the costs: eight residents could perhaps get along with one bathroom, but twelve people would require two baths.

A larger number of people would also put more wear and tear on every room in the house, especially the bathrooms and kitchens.

In general, the rooms in the home should be adequate in size to suit their purpose. Sunshine, bright rooms, and a homey atmosphere are as necessary in a community residence as they are in any house, perhaps even more essential. Surfaces should show dirt easily and be easily cleanable (e.g., vinyl wallpaper, semi-gloss paint, and no shag rugs). These surfaces should also be as durable as possible within the confines of "hominess."

The kitchen is the center attraction in a community residence, just as it is in any house, but special considerations are in order because of the larger number of people using it, sometimes for every conceivable purpose. There should be an ample amount of cabinet space for all the food, dishes, utensils, and so forth; there should be room enough for a large stove and refrigerator; there should be plenty of counter space for several people to work at a time as well as space for a breakfast–snack table. There should also be plenty of move-around room. The surfaces in the kitchen take a considerable beating, especially if people are to eat breakfasts and snacks there. The floor should be an excellent quality, easy-to-clean, scuff-proof type because a minimum of twelve people will be walking on it daily and likely dropping eggs and gravy on it. The countertops should be formica and seamless, and the color should be light enough to show dirt easily. Walls, and cabinets should be as durable as possible and easily washable. In planning the kitchen, as much as possible should be done to make it dirt-and-wear resistant before the residents move in.

The bathrooms in a community residence also receive a great deal of use, and many of the same considerations pertinent to the kitchen apply to the bathroom. Ceramic tile is a very durable bathtub wall, and a good flooring and washable walls other than the tile area are very necessary for durability and cleanliness. If the bathroom in an older house has tiles, cracks around the tub and basin will likely need to be caulked so that no water can leak behind them. Any cracks in the flooring around the toilet and tub will also need to be sealed. Since this room is going to be used by many people, extra towel racks, medicine chests, and so forth are very helpful. Like the kitchen, as much as possible should be done to make the bathrooms durable before the residents move in.

The bedrooms should be as homey as possible. They should also be adequate in space and furnishings. Double rooms are most common, but if singles are possible, the privacy and responsibility they provide are very helpful to programming. Most institutionalized people have had no private space to identify as their own. Their bedrooms may be their first experience in creating and then living with their creations. These bedrooms should have adequate floor space consistent with building codes, and each should have adequate closet space. In each bedroom, the number of electrical outlets as well as lighting fixtures, both of which are costly to add, should be sufficient to meet the needs of the number of planned occupants. Many older homes have a minimal number of electrical outlets per room, and current building codes may require a certain number per room or per foot of wallspace.

The living room, dining room, and recreation room are all very similar, and some general comments can suffice for all three. Electrical service should be checked in these rooms as in the bedrooms. At least one of the rooms should be large enough to hold comfortably the expected population of the house for meetings and parties.

In general, utilities in the house can be very expensive to renovate, replace, or install, so a careful examination of these systems with an eye to house requirements is essential. First of all, local building code requirements should be listed and then determinations made of what is needed within these codes. In many areas the codes need not be strictly adhered to unless major renovations are to be made in the house. The building inspector in the town or city can be very helpful in interpreting these codes. (A note: the building inspector will have to inspect the house at some point and either issue a license directly or make recommendations to a zoning or licensing board, so his support is essential, preferably, as mentioned in a previous chapter, as a member of the board of directors. More about him later in this chapter.)

The plumbing in a house can appear very straightforward, but there may be some problems. For example, the hot water supply may not be sufficient for a great deal of usage. Will the hot water flow suffice for five or six baths in one hour? If not, renting a water heater is relatively inexpensive, and if funds are sufficient, a big, fifty-gallon, quick reclamation tank is best. Overall, copper is the ideal plumbing material. However, grey-colored pipes probably aren't lead, but an alloy metal. This alloy is fine if the present water system is adequate, but it can cause problems if any changes in the overall plumbing system have to be made.

The electrical system, which can also produce some problems, should be considered. Local building codes come into play here in that additional service, for example, can be very expensive if new systems have to be put behind walls. In the cellar, one or two or three different types of wiring could be visible overhead. The first type is wire covered only with fabric; this is a very old system. It will probably look frayed and will probably be noticed by the building inspector since it is very unsafe and could cause shorts or even fires. The second system is called knob and tube. This looks like a strand of metal coiled into a tube, and it is much safer than the first type and presents few if any problems. The third and newest type is the plastic coated wire. This is an excellent system and is generally problem free. The fuse box is also important in considering the electrical system.

Additions of any kind will have to start at the box. The lines into the house may not be adequate to provide additional services, and it may be necessary to increase them before adding any new circuits. This is especially true if washer–dryer outlets or electric stove service have to be added. To put in a new fuse box for any additional service is more costly than running a wire from an adequate box to the new outlet. The adequacy of service is measured in amperes, and the number of amperes required to operate additional appliances can be found on the metal tags on each appliance being added. A comparison with the box will tell whether sufficient amperes of service are available (not being used by some other circuit) for these appliances. If a whole new box is needed, this cost is worth considering, and a professional electrician should be consulted.

The heating system is very difficult to discuss in any great detail because of the various kinds of systems available and the different fuels that can be used. A few comments from experience might be helpful. In a hot water system, water for domestic use might come from a continuous flow unit built into the boiler itself. There are many pros and cons about this method of water heating, but in most cases, this type of system will not be adequate to supply the hot water needed by a group of twelve or more people. The radiators in a steam system may heat very unevenly (i.e., the radiator in one room might be hot, while the radiator in the next room is stone cold), but this problem can be remedied by installing adjustable valves to control the flow of steam into the individual radiators. A hot air system provides very dry heat. This can be remedied by attaching a humidifier to the system or by using a large portable humidifier. Adequate humidification is primarily a public health measure for it reduces the number and severity of respiratory illnesses. It also saves money in heating costs and adds to the life of furniture by keeping it from drying out and separating.

Mortgaging and Leasing

The financing of a community residence is a problem with a number of options. Each of the various alternatives have advantages and disadvantages, but one disadvantage of most is time. Thus, once the choice of home has been made, a method of financing should be developed as soon as possible. The financing of a house can be done in any number of ways, which means that any arrangement that suits the situation can be satisfactory. Aggressiveness and wheeling and dealing with potential backers is in order.

Basically there are two ways of obtaining a house. The first is a lease or rental plan and the second is an ownership situation. The first type usually implies less responsibility but may be more expensive and more tenuous, since the landlord can terminate the relationship at will. Ownership is more stable and less expensive, but it entails more responsibility for the house. In addition, purchasing a home requires downpayment capital that might well be used some place else.

A lease agreement is basically an agreement made with an owner of a property to utilize that property for a period of time. There are a variety of finer details involved in a lease, and these usually provide the basic fodder for negotiations. These details include utilities, renovation costs, option to purchase, taxes, repairs and maintenance, term of the lease with options, and of course that old standby, dollars. In putting together an idea of what is a reasonable lease, a group seeking a community home should look at all of these details with respect to its start-up position. For example, while there may be little cash available at the time of the lease signing, delayed funding from various agencies may be forthcoming. In this case, then, a lease might be in terms of an option to purchase at an agreed upon price (less can always be offered) with a percentage of the monthly rent going towards the purchase price. If this is the case, it might be worthwhile to pay extra on a monthly basis to have the landlord do as many renovations as possible. Because there are so many possible arrangements, the best advice for prospective community home organizers is to sit, think, talk, and seek professional advice on as many of the options as are available. In any given situation, the goal should be to work out the most advantageous way to put the lease together.

Owning a house presents a somewhat different situation. Mortgaging money is very tight and very expensive now, which makes buying a house difficult. Most banks are asking for a 20 percent downpayment, and even that does not guarantee receipt of the loan. Even when a loan is secured, interest rates are incredibly high, making any loan more expensive. However, a mortgage is still less expensive than a lease. Monthly mortgage payments build up money against the loan, which is not the case when they are paid to a landlord, and this amount could perhaps be borrowed against at a later date. Also, any renovations or repairs made on the house enhance its value, but conversely there is no landlord to absorb the cost of them. Perhaps one of the most important advantages for buying as opposed to leasing is the property tax abatement available to a non-profit corporation with tax-exempt status. This can provide a substantial savings over a lease situation in which the landlord has to pay the property taxes by passing on the cost. There are a number of alternative methods to use in funding a house. These methods involve a great deal of work, and perhaps some expertise and contacts with knowledgeable people.

The first method involves using the local housing authority or its local corollary. In Massachusetts, Housing Authority people are able to help in a variety of ways. First, there is a rental assistance program in which the authority leases a house and then subleases it to the community home group for an amount based upon the income of the residents. Secondly, the authority can buy a house outright, renovate it, and then rent it under the same conditions as above. Thirdly, and perhaps best, the authority can build a suitable new house and also rent that to the group. This latter takes a long time; at least two years may be required before moving into such a new house. The housing authority may be able to build a community residence as part of a project for the elderly or a low-income project, but it does not have to be located on the same site as these projects. In general, local housing authorities, which are composed of people from within the community and which usually function autonomously, can be very helpful in launching community programs.

A second funding source is the Housing and Urban Development department of the federal government, which has regional offices in or near most local areas. A variety of programs are available through this agency, and one of them may meet the needs of a particular local situation. Other potential sources of funding include local Associations for Retarded Citizens, philanthropic organizations, and perhaps county or local government agencies.

In any case, it is essential when seeking funds for a house to be well organized. Potential backers are going to want to know all about the program: numbers, services, staffing, other funding, starting date, ad infinitum. Furthermore, when looking for a grant or working with different government organizations, prior knowledge of the types of programs for which funds are available can assure that the request approximates the requirements. For example, if funding is available for programs for physically handicapped people, they might be easily integrated into a community home program with just some minor renovations to a bedroom and a bathroom. By incorporating these people into the program and providing services for them, community home organizers may be eligible for the funds. The initial program can remain essentially the same, but the slight revisions can make all the funding and the entire program possible.

Constraints

There are a variety of different safety codes, guidelines, and procedures that may be required by different local, county, state, and even federal agencies. These regulations are very different in different towns and states and would be almost impossible to spell out in any great detail. Some general comments should suffice.

Fire Laws

Fire laws vary, but there are some general issues that seem common to all. An adequate number of fire extinguishers is the first consideration. In our situation, a five pound CO_2 extinguisher in the kitchen and two water-filled, air-pressure-powered extinguishers in other parts of the house were sufficient. The latter are inexpensive to maintain (they can be filled to 100 psi at a gas station just like a tire), inexpensive to buy, easy to use, and are generally a sound investment. If they are not already red (some codes call for this), red tape will make them easy to identify. A smoke or heat detection device is relatively inexpensive and very worthwhile. There are battery operated ones available from Sears & Roebuck that seem to be adequate. Also, there should be two means of egress from every floor above the first floor; a back stairway is usually there, but if not, a fire ladder is relatively inexpensive. An emergency light may be necessary also and can be very useful. All of these devices are nice gifts—or fund-raising objectives —for local organizations eager to contribute something to the house.

Building Codes

Building codes often call for some distinct specifications in the structure of the house. These should be studied carefully by a knowledgeable person because many older homes don't comply, and some renovations would be almost impossible. The requirements involve things like width of hallways, width of stairways, size of doorways, both means of egress needing to be straight stairways, and so forth. Here again, the building inspector can be very helpful in dealing with these restrictions.

The building inspector is a very important asset to a group trying to locate and establish a community residence. There are several reasons for his importance, some official and some unofficial. He can help in avoiding many problems, but if he is opposed to the project, he can be a real problem.

His official duties include the inspection of buildings and the issuance of building permits, certificates of occupancy, or licenses. Within these capacities, he can obviously be a very helpful individual. He has to inspect any house according to the building codes that cover wiring, plumbing, structure, and safety features. Many older buildings do not comply with all the codes (i.e., many older plumbing features are no longer acceptable under present standards), and he can either require changes in all substandard aspects of the house or he can use his discretion and find them acceptable. He has to issue a certificate of occupancy on the property for its intended use and either issue a license or make a recommendation to the licensing board. Finally, he would be involved in a hearing of a zoning Board of Appeals; he would report on the suitability of the building and make a recommendation. It is very easy to see his importance in a solely official way.

Many times the building inspector has unofficial powers that are equally important. A wink or a scowl at the Zoning Board of Appeals hearing is an obvious example. But further, he is involved in the building trades in many ways, and can therefore be helpful in interpreting zoning laws, suggesting the best ways to make renovations and repairs, and helping to get things done at the best price. As mentioned, he is probably a good man to have on the board of directors, if this doesn't constitute a conflict of interest. Although the procedures that are followed in different areas do vary, the building inspector can be considered a powerful person within any structure.

Regulatory Agencies

There are other standards that may have to be maintained in a community residence. These will vary with the type of persons to be served, the funding source, and the various state agencies. To go into detail would be impossible here, but some general comments about these regulatory agencies, and how to find out about them from the start might be helpful.

Various state Departments of Mental Health, or their corollaries, usually have standards for both fire and safety as well as program. Following the standards is especially important if funding is being made by these departments. Additional standards may also be required by other involved agencies such as the Department of Public Health and the Office for Children. Surprisingly enough, these different agencies probably have no communication with each other, and certainly no coordinated standards, which is a very sad commentary on bureaucracies. If the home is financed through a local housing authority, its codes and procedures will also have to be followed.

Another whole problem is thrown in when the state tries to get reimbursed through Title XIX funds, which are essentially Medicaid monies paid to the state for certain services. The federal government sets standards for projects if they are to be eligible for reimbursement through this program. Since these standards are very strict with regard to structures, trying to follow them may make finding a house very difficult. Here again, prior knowledge from the state agency is best.

The need for such standards is very important in community residence programs. Many very poorly-run projects have given the whole movement a bad name in the past. These standards, then, could be very constructive and informative, and hopefully, changes in the whole process of monitoring and evaluating programs will lead to a healthier situation that would eliminate inequities in programming and funding.

Zoning

Zoning is a very ticklish issue that, first of all, requires the services of a lawyer. (Again, having a lawyer on the board of directors is desirable since he can provide legal services and advice for such other legal issues as real estate closings and lease writing.) Zoning laws vary in each town, and procedures and costs vary also. There are entirely different categories and definitions in each town, so a set of zoning laws in one town may have nothing in common with the zoning laws of an adjacent town. There also may be different delay factors involved such as time of public notice, allowable deliberation time for the board, and so forth. Further, the costs may vary, the application forms may vary in the amount of work and time required, and local political scenes may call for entirely different strategies. In general, zoning boards are very important, but problems with them are difficult to predict.

The rule of being well-organized really applies here. At a board hearing, the project's representatives must know as much as possible about the program as well as the zoning boards requirements. For example, zoning officials may ask questions about parking, sewage, the nearest fire hydrant, or even the number of dogs to be kept. If trouble from the zoning board is anticipated, role-playing a hearing situation with as many tough questions as can be conceived will benefit those who will represent the organizing group at the actual hearing. After a zoning board denial, the court is the only recourse, and since this is a long and expensive process, the hearing and consequent ruling are both very important from the outset. Finally, it is advisable to investigate the possibility of getting a variance or permit even though the home's location is in compliance with the zoning laws and an appeal need not be made. This is insurance against someone complaining to the Zoning Board of Appeals later and questioning the home's right to be located where it is. Once the Zoning Board of Appeals has approved a location, the only recourse a future antagonist would have would be the courts, which is expensive and time-consuming for him.

Furniture and Equipment, Renovations, and Location

The furniture and equipment in a community residence is a considerable expense. It must be homey in appearance and yet be useful and durable.

These requirements make this a problem that deserves some discussion. First, we will deal with some general principles about furniture requirements and then present some ideas for individual rooms.

When looking for furnishings, appliances, and so forth, it should be kept in mind that a home is being created for people who perhaps have never had a home or have not lived in one for many years. They will feel most comfortable in the "homiest" kind of environment since they have lived in an institutional world of chrome, plastic, and metal furnishings. Thus, there is a need to stay as far away from these things as possible and to choose warm colors, dark woods, fabrics rather than plastic for upholstery, rugs rather than tiles. From our experience, a homelike atmosphere is most easily created with colonial furniture, but the same effects can be achieved with more modern or contemporary furnishings.

The institutional chrome, plastic, and metal furnishings mentioned above have taught residents nothing about caring for their environment. It makes no difference where you put out a cigarette or spill a coke when you live in a cement-walled, tile-floored, plastic-furnitured environment. Therefore, residents of the community home may be a little harder on their surroundings than might be expected of non-institutionalized people. However, there are kinds of fabric coverings and surfaces for use in the home that will stand up to such abuse. Nylon, herculon, and polyurethane are good examples of materials that are homey and durable too.

Equipment is an especially difficult area. The residents will probably be learning how to use appliances while they are in the house. Dials will be turned the wrong way, stove burners will be left on, the refrigerator door will flap and be left open, and the garbage disposal will be fed various and sundry non-edible items. It is necessary to buy quality equipment that will live through this kind of treatment, and it is also worthwhile choosing appliances with the simplest operating procedures possible.

The Kitchen

The kitchen needs a great deal of discussion with respect to furniture and equipment. There are many special needs here because of the number and type of people to be served. Basic is the kitchen table, which has to fit into the kitchen and still leave ample room to move around. Since it will probably not seat more than four or perhaps six people, the kitchen table can be used for serving breakfast or a cup of coffee but not the meals in which everyone is to be seated together. Used maple sets, which are usually easy to find, seem to be substantial. The chrome ones don't stand up to heavy wear very well and do not look as homey.

The appliances especially the stove and the dishwasher, should be of the large variety. The refrigerator should be frostfree and easy to clean. In our experience, two refrigerators in the house, both with large freezer space on top or side, have worked well since meat and other perishables can be bought in bulk quantities more cheaply. Two refrigerators also provide other opportunities. One refrigerator can be kept in the kitchen and the other in a back pantry, the cellar or some out of the way place. Daily food can be placed in the kitchen refrigerator; reserves can be stored in the out of the way one. Whenever buying any appliance, it is wise to buy the best quality possible because an inexpensive dishwasher that lasts only two years does not save money.

In sum, the kitchen should be well planned in all its aspects because this room will be the focal point of the community residence. If it runs well and stands up, half the problems of running the home will be resolved.

The Dining Room

Dining room furniture is pretty straightforward. Twelve to fifteen chairs are necessary. Whatever the number, there must be enough for everyone. Durability and comfort should be considered since they can be used all over the house for groups getting together or other special needs. We were lucky to get a great buy on hardrock pegged and wedged chairs that are very substantial. If possible, imported, stapled, particle-board type of construction should be avoided for these simply will not last. Pine also doesn't hold up as well as it should.

Dining room tables are an interesting problem. There are a wide variety of options: square ones to seat four, round ones of all sizes, or long thin ones that seat everyone. An inexpensive, but sturdy one that fits the dining room is the best choice. We have built all of our tables from scratch, and they have lasted well. They are nine feet long and four feet wide, have crossbuck legs, and are finished with polyurethane. Such tables are very easy and cheap to build and should be considered in view of the difficulties of finding a long, large table at a reasonable price. In any case, however, purchasing or building the dining table would make a good project for local groups wishing to contribute to the project. In addition to the table, a sideboard adds a nice home-like touch to the dining room and conveniently holds a twenty-cup coffee pot.

The dining room floor is really going to take a lot of spills. Paint or linoleum will suffice, but treated hardwood floors are just as practical and look very nice. Polyurethane is a good, durable finish. Overall, the dining room can be one of the most attractive rooms in the house, so a little effort on curtains and furnishings is not wasted.

Living and Recreation Rooms

The living room and the recreation room can become a variety of things. A den or a TV room are just two of the alternatives. Whatever the choices, however, smoking should be restricted in one of the rooms for the comfort and health of others.

Furnishings can be suited to any budget. A new elegant three piece set is very nice, but more expensive than used furniture that has withstood the test of time and comfort. The important thing is that both of these rooms be attractive, warm, and homey. A piano will always be used; a fish tank will be appreciated; flowers, plants, bookcases, and stereos are possible and often desirable accessories that nevertheless require resources and imagination. Lastly, one of these rooms must be large enough to hold a large group meeting or an occassional party.

Renovations

Renovations are difficult to discuss in any great detail, but they are important and can be considered in some general ways. Most important, renovations have a tendency to increase in scope as work on the project progresses. A small job like replacing a linoleum floor can suddenly involve new subflooring, a couple of new floor joists, new mop boards, and so on. Thus, a sixty-dollar afternoon job becomes a three-hundred-dollar five-day saga. A good way to handle unforseen possibilities is to take a hard look at what needs to be done, and then at what might have to be done, and then plan on the second estimate.

When looking at a house as a buyer, renovations should be taken into account in considering the costs since it is often possible to have major renovations amortised in the mortgage. When looking as a lessee, renovations become good bargaining cards. When dealing with a housing authority or a state agency, they should pay for as much as they can. Renovations also make good projects for interested groups; the local men's club, for instance, could pay for new plumbing or for having a wall removed.

Most importantly, all aspects of planning renovations must be studied carefully. What really needs to be done? Can it be done? How much will it cost? When can it be done? Who can do it? This might be a good place to mention that having at least one person on the staff who has a little know-how in renovations and maintenance can save many dollars.

Location

In the search for a residence, location is of primary importance. The most important consideration in terms of location is what is available outside of the house in a particular neighborhood or area. Transportation plays a crucial role in this decision because a bus or mass transit system makes a larger number of services available. A van or other vehicle increases mobility, but takes up staff time. Walking has proven itself to be the number one mode of transportation among our residents in a semi-urbanized city of 30,000. Thus, each of our community homes are located within walking distance of movies, the YMCA, shopping areas, churches, and so forth. Although we also have a fifteen-passenger van to use for trips, accessability basically means within walking distance.

Another "location" consideration is the type of neighborhood. There are of course some monetary constraints that come into play as well as some minimum standards concerning structure. But within the general run of houses and neighborhoods, some characteristics are more desirable than others. We have found large house lots and yards to be advantageous and closeness to other houses a drawback. However, a mansion in the hills is a mini-institution, and even though the breathing space needed for a group of twelve people is quite large and might run into a neighbor's yard, there seem to be definite advantages to being in a neighborhood. A mixed neighborhood—one with apartments, one-family dwellings, older and younger people, and transient as well as permanent neighbors is even better since these people are much more tolerant of different lifestyles and different people. They also seem to be freer in expressing their opinions and feelings concerning new neighbors.

Conclusion

Taken together, all of the factors discussed in this chapter make it very difficult to see any orderly and clear progression of events from the time a group decides it wants to open a community residence to the day the first resident walks through the door. Let's talk about some of these variables as a progression and put them in some kind of temporal relationship.

People wanting to create a community residence is the first and most important step. They can get together through an Association for Retarded Citizens or a parents meeting or a city group, such as the Chamber of Commerce or Jaycees. After the decision to go ahead has been made, the first thing the group must do is incorporate.

The next steps in the sequence involve study and research: visiting other groups, seeing what kinds of programs are being run, finding out where the funding is being obtained. Since it is very necessary for the group to think in terms of an entire program for the people to be taken into the home, day programs, mental health services in the area, and other facilities that would be available for the residents should be considered carefully.

At this point, it will be necessary for the initiators to begin raising capital and hiring some staff. The hard, tedious work of negotiating agreements for funding, furniture, housing, hiring full staff, and so forth are all imminent, and someone must assume full-time responsibility for it. Although some local group may have a paid staff person who can take on some of these duties, which would save on some costs, the stage of development is now beyond the scope of volunteerism.

An administrative type of person should be hired to start the program on a solid basis. Seeking sources of funding is a necessary point of departure for his duties. At the same time, he should also be learning about the housing market, trying to secure funds for furniture and a vehicle, finding out about zoning, building codes, and so forth. In addition, he can be doing some public relations, creating liaisons in the community, negotiating with the institution about the kind of population to be served, and discussing how the institution will relate to the residence. This second phase is a process of feeling out and creating some favorable situations without making any firm commitments. It comes to an abrupt end when the funding is secured, and a funding date is definite.

The final phase is moving ahead and making a commitment—on a population first, then on a house, a staff, and a family dog. The staff becomes in many ways the focus now, and they should be involved in setting up the house and selecting the residents.

To put some of the characteristics of the house in relative positions of importance would be hopeless, but perhaps some anecdotal comments might prove helpful. A house that is too small is too small! Yes, it is cheaper, but the program will pay dearly for it in the long run: three people just do not fit in that bedroom; having only one room for the houseparents will cost six months of each set of houseparents' stay, and that is very expensive.

On location: being accessible to the community is crucial to programming, for the more difficult it is to get around, the easier it is to set up a mini-institution. Walking distance is very important. A large yard is nice, but as long as people have room to sit outside and move around a little, central location is a more important condition.

On the home itself: prepare the house as much as possible before the residents move in. This is when the staff has the most time, and when start-up monies are most available.

A personal word of encouragement: we have been involved in the opening of seven houses, but we have no magic tricks to share. We have made some mistakes along the road, but our houses are open and successful. Things like this just do not fail. They get delayed, confused, perhaps even hopeless in appearance, but they do not fail.

A final plea to prospective community home organizers: think about everything as much as you can and make all decisions carefully. You are taking on a thrilling and weighty challenge. People will change and grow right in front of you, if you do it right.

4

Liaison with the Community and Community Services
William P. Gerry

The notion of interaction with the community by the staff and residents of a community residence can be seen as a two-fold problem: making the community in all its aspects available to the people and getting the people into the community. There are many aspects to the community, but this discussion will consider only such available services as health, financial, recreational, and social resources of the community. The idea of getting people out of the house and into the community is primarily a programmatic concern, but it also has some administrative and financial implications. The problem of making resources and services available to the residents is one of creating liaisons with the various people and organizations of the community who deal in these services.

Many of the community services that are essential to a well-run program are bureaucratic in nature. Success in dealing with these bureaucracies requires learning certain basic skills, for as bureaucracies increase in size and become more diversified, their original function can become lost in the mire of bureaucratic detail, worker alienation, misprogrammed computers, and dead files. Here then are some general rules that when followed, can help clear the way through the bureaucratic jungles.

First General Rule. Select an appropriate individual in the bureaucracy and make face-to-face contact with that person. Know his name; tell him about the program; find out about the workings of the bureaucracy from this person; even take him to dinner. Then, use that person for all programs dealings with that bureaucracy: send all records, applications, complaints, and so forth directly to him. In sum, consider that one person the only person at the bureaucracy.

Second General Rule. Do everything necessary for the bureaucracy to be able to do its job. Make sure that the bureaucracy has all of the information it needs, and be aware of both the rights and responsibilities under the law of all parties concerned. Many times after a three-month delay a bureaucrat will say, "But we haven't received that person's birthdate as yet." Do everything possible to make sure this type of situation never happens. Never leave any loose ends and expect a bureaucrat to make a phone call if something needs clarification; he won't do it.

Third General Rule. Find out how the bureaucracy works and watchdog everything through the system. Know what desks things must cross and which people make decisions. Use whatever methods are necessary to make sure all things occur.

Fourth General Rule. Expect delays. Any bureaucracy takes time to work even under optimum conditions. Anticipate these delays and plan for them. This is hard to do when two or three bureaucracies work together in a chain effect, but careful planning and follow-up methods can avoid many problems caused by bureaucratic delays.

Fifth General Rule. Bureaucrats are people who have opted for a secure and uneventful occupation. Like the residents in a community home, they respond to both positive and negative reinforcement. Therefore, if a bureaucrat is not working satisfactorily, threaten to call his superior, put a letter in the newspaper, and so forth.

Sixth General Rule. Whenever a bureaucrat makes any kind of a commitment, get it in writing. It is very easy for a bureaucrat to say yes, but he may be hesitant to put any kind of commitment in writing. One way to overcome this problem is to write a summary letter of a phone conversation or a meeting, and then send copies of it to all interested parties. This puts the commitment in writing without the bureaucrat having to do it.

Seventh General Rule. Don't let bureaucrats blame a computer for a delay or an error. A computer has never made a mistake; people make mistakes. "The computer broke down" is a bureaucratic stall that should be ignored or rejected.

Eighth General Rule. Many bureaucrats who are responsible for making decisions seem to post guards to protect them from people who want them to make decisions. (Remember, a bureaucrat who is worried about his position knows that if he doesn't do anything, he doesn't do anything wrong.) These guards can be secretaries, assistants, or other underlings who can listen to problems but can give no answers; they are put there to discuss a given situation assuasively but without making any kind of commitment. Do not accept these people as decision makers or even reliable liasons; talk only to the person who can make the decision.

Ninth General Rule. A meeting is a bureaucratic timewaster. Some are useful and necessary, but many, especially those called by bureaucrats, are senseless. Try to avoid them and make a phone call suffice. When it is absolutely necessary to have a meeting, there seems to be an unwritten bureaucratic law that it should take place at their office, and last at least an hour. After twenty minutes, never be afraid to say "Well, if that's all there is to discuss, I have other things to get to." This tactic is also good negative reinforcement for bureaucrats who have nothing better to do than waste time with meetings.

Institutions

The first aspect of community and bureaucracy likely to be encountered is the institution. The purpose of the community home program is to get people out of the institution, and the relationship with the institution is very important since its staff can be very helpful, or difficult. Many staff members at the institution will care a great deal about the welfare of the residents and be very concerned about where they are placed. Their feelings may even be "parental" in nature, and they may feel guarded about another group or program saying, in effect, "We can do a better job of providing for this person." (More about this in the section on parents.) The institution can do much of the administrative work: it can provide information that is helpful in programming; it can supply staff or professional help.

The relationship between the community home and the institutional staff is very involved, and every aspect of this relationship should be discussed with them at an early stage in the development of a program. Specific information about the program should be in terms of the type of people suitable for the program, the types of day programs and services to be offered, and any limitations on the types of people that can be accepted (epileptics or the physically handicapped, for example).

Arrangements should be made for a system of referral and for decision making concerning the selection of residents, particularly the amount and kind of information to be received from them before any decision is made about a particular person coming into the program. This could include medical information, a background summary, information on special needs such as speech therapy, and some idea of the functional ability of the individual. Test scores are not necessary for they tell practically nothing about a person's functional ability—we have had several "severely retarded" people be quite successful in our program, and several "very intelligent" people be troublesome to our staff and very unsuccessful in the program. The selection process should also involve a personal interview with a member of the program's staff as well as a procedure for allowing prospective residents to visit the house prior to possible entrance into the program. Arranging clear lines of communication during the time a resident is in the house and determining conditions for the return of residents to the institution if they are unsuccessful will save time and trouble should such a situation arise.

It is best to find out what kinds of help the institution can offer for professional services (such as medication, speech, physical and occupational therapy), but having the residents return to the institution for these services should be avoided if at all possible. Speech and occupational therapy can be available in the house, or better still, at some other place in the community. Perhaps the institution can provide a job slot for an assistant or some other essential staff. However, although the institution can be a resource of great value, it is still an institution, complete with bureaucracy, inadequacy, and red tape, and therefore, should be relied on for only those things it can actually do.

Local, State, and Federal Agencies

The financial situation of the residents is essential to the success of the program. It is almost always essential to collect a weekly or monthly rent from each resident. In addition, they must have some money available for personal use. There are four possible sources of income for the residents. These include income from a job; a built-up bank account from Social Security payments; Supplemental Security Income; welfare or general relief.

A resident working a full-time competitive job in the community is the ultimate arrangement. He can pay his way both in the house and in the community with very few administrative hassles for the staff and can also be a tremendous programmatic influence. However, even though employed, a resident may still be eligible for some benefits. Depending on income or survivors' benefits available through the Social Security Administration, he may be eligible for Medicaid, Medicare, and/or payments through Social Security. Finding out about these sources may enable a person to save some money for moving into a more independent living situation, getting a car, or taking a vacation. Thus, although a person working full-time is his own major source of income, he may still be eligible for benefits.

The second form of income would be from a bank account of considerable proportion. This could be an inheritance, a trust fund, a backlog of many years of unused Social Security payments, or an account built up while working in the institution. This usually presents no problem, but there could be a few difficulties. The institution may have the money in an account at its local bank, and it may want to control the money through a social worker. This means that every month or two, a social worker must request money from someone, then pass it on to the individual. A social worker who is forgetful or busy can cause delays in the receipt of the money or could try to dictate its use. This situation can be avoided by requesting large sums for long intervals and by sending in requests well in advance of the actual need for it.

Executors of trusts can often create similar delays, but there are several ways of getting necessary funds for the resident from these people. The first method involves emotional appeals: the best interests of the resident at the heart of the matter; a system for getting money from them will lessen their work and make things easier for everyone; their withholding the money is keeping the resident from having certain opportunities or luxuries such as a TV, a stereo, a vacation, or some new clothes! If all this fails to get the funds released, the second method would be to threaten a legal action. It is very clear in the law that an individual is competent unless he is shown incompetent and that he can both receive his own social security benefits directly and remove his money at any time from a state institution unless he has been shown to be incompetent. This type of action does require a lawyer, and although it may sound harsh, the money question is a difficult one that often warrants such measures.

A major goal of most rehabilitation counselors in the institution is the creation of a bank account for the resident that then becomes a sacred cow —a rainy day fund that allows for no rainy days. They may also express concern that the resident has not demonstrated his ability to live in the community and therefore might return, so it would be best to keep the money for a while. There are probably many factors that make social workers at institutions reluctant to release money, but whatever the reason, it is generally inappropriate.

Families are an even stickier issue. It seems quite evident, unfortunately, that many family members try to conserve the money so that they can get it when the resident dies. Furthermore, family members may often feel that retarded people do not have the same needs as normal people: their clothing doesn't have to be as nice; they don't need a television or a vacation; somehow their life is less expensive than that of others. Perhaps this is a little overstated, and to be sure, many families are very concerned, warm, helpful, and merely frugal. No matter what the reasons, it is often necessary to obtain from them whatever money is necessary for the resident to live in an increasingly expensive world.

The Social Security Administration is probably going to be the major source of income for most residents of the community home. It is also the most massive bureaucracy the staff will have to deal with, since there are many different types of benefits that could be utilized by the residents. In Massachusetts, Supplemental Security Income has replaced what used to be called Disability Assistance; Medicaid (based primarily on a person's eligibility for SSI benefits), Medicare, and some low-cost health insurance policies round out the field of Social Security benefits that we have seen. There may be other possibilities with which we are not familiar, but local Social Security offices can provide information about these.

There is a long delay built into any Social Security related income. A minimum waiting period of two months can be expected. Therefore, applications should be sent into the "process" as soon as possible. Since these applications are very long and difficult to fill out and require medical and administrative information, they should be completed by the staff or personnel at the institution prior to the resident moving into the program. If a resident had been receiving benefits while at the institution, a change of mailing address should be filed as soon as possible.

The Welfare Department in Massachusetts performs two functions that can be helpful. It pays general relief, and it administers Medicaid. General relief should be sought for an individual only after he or she has been denied SSI (which could happen under the existing eligibility requirements). General relief should be applied for as soon as there seems to be trouble with an SSI application. The intake interview may not be held for several weeks after an appointment has been made, but payments would be retroactive to the date the appointment was made. In any event, the SSI problem should be resolved before the appointment with the Welfare Department. Medicaid is administered through the Welfare Department upon receipt of notification of eligibility for SSI, at which point the Welfare Department automatically issues a Medicaid number as well as a form letter, to be given to billers, stating that the bearer is eligible for Medicaid and that payments will be made retroactive to the time of application for SSI. As with the Social Security Administration, Welfare may be able to help in other ways.

There are other bureaucracies that can be of assistance to the program or the residents. These will be mentioned here under their Massachusetts titles, but the corollaries in other states may exist under different names. The Department of Mental Health provides funding on a contractual basis for the operation of community residences; it also administers the state institutions. The Massachusetts Rehabilitation Commission funds training and evaluation programs for day programming. The Division of Employment Security pays benefits to unemployed persons under certain conditions and may prove helpful as a job placement agency. It also may administer or know the whereabouts of vocational and rehabilitation programs that might be of help. The Veteran's Administration provides a complete list of services for veterans. The list could go on endlessly: Massachusetts Commission for the Blind, H.E.W. in all its different aspects, the local Housing Authority, and the Department of Public Health, just to name a few.

Medical Services

Health services are an essential part of the community home program. In order to change behaviors and teach skills, one must have healthy people. Institutions often provide inadequate health care and maintain inadequate records of that care. Therefore, it is necessary to consider physical exams and consequent medical attentions as a first part of the programming. A complete physical should include an eye and ear examination and, perhaps, neurological testing. A format for these services should be set up before the people come into the program and arrangements should be made with local physicians, dentists, and ophthalmologists to see all of the residents once they have come into the house. Other specialists could be contacted when needed or perhaps the physician can make a referral when necessary. These health services should be paid for through Medicaid for most people, but some residents may have Medicare or a private health insurance plan. As mentioned, the resident need not have a Medicaid number to receive services under the plan. As long as the appropriate agency has been contacted and issued a letter stating that the person has applied for and will receive these benefits and that retroactive payments will be made, most professionals are willing to cooperate since payment will ultimately be made to them.

Special Services

Special needs such as speech, physical, and occupational therapy can present some special problems. In our particular area we are blessed with three mental health institutions, five colleges, and a school for the deaf. This means that speech and physical therapists are available in the area on a part-time consulting basis. Other areas of Massachusetts and the country may not be as fortunate. However, there will usually be some place within hailing distance that offers services like these. A hospital or a school may very well offer these services and have trained staff people available. The method of receiving services can be arranged in several ways. Arrangements can be made directly with the individual therapist for his services, or they can be made through the hospital or school by paying it the fee for services performed during a staff therapist's regular workday. Which plan is better depends on the situation. Perhaps the hospital or school does not have a full workload for the therapist and therefore could offer an attractive deal just to keep the therapist busy. On the other hand, a benevolent therapist may volunteer his services, especially if the program needs are minimal. In any event, the arrangements concerning whatever special services might be needed should be made prior to the opening of the house. The availability of these services are sometimes required for eligibility for certain types of funding.

A psychological consultant is an important person in the program. We have been very fortunate in having available a psychologist with an excellent background and working knowledge of programming and training methods. A number of very essential functions can be performed by a well-trained psychologist. The most direct input he would have is in the development of individual goals and training programs or behavioral techniques to be utilized by the staff in achieving these goals. A second function concommitant with the first is the training of staff members in these various behavioral techniques. A third function is the on-going evaluation and updating of individual goals and training methods as residents achieve certain behavioral goals, or as various methods lose effectiveness or prove unsuccessful. A fourth function is one of troubleshooting as difficulties arise. These may range from a serious argument between two residents to staff disagreements concerning programming. Situations like these emphasize the importance of a consultant role as opposed to a staff role. A consultant is not in the pecking order of the staff, nor is he or she working exclusively for one organization. This puts the consultant in the ideal position of being able to remain outside the day-to-day affairs of the house and thus being able to step in with a somewhat more objective perspective on a given situation. This can be compared to the vantage point of a referee in a sporting event: he is not a member of the team, doesn't win or lose anything, and will go home after the game to another job or interest.

An effective trained consultant is a very essential part of any viable, dynamic program. The psychologist should be one of the first people hired for the program for he will be helpful in hiring and training staff and setting up general programmatic concepts. There are several ways of arranging for a consultant's services: an hourly rate of payment, a session rate of payment, or perhaps some flat fee on a weekly or monthly basis. Whatever the arrangement, this person must be chosen relatively early in the development of the program, and steps should be taken to assure that a person with the necessary background, training, and abilities is retained.

Perhaps the most important liaisons involved in the program will be those with the people in charge of the day activities of your residents. Day activities could be a school setting, a developmental day care center, a sheltered workshop, or some form of competitive employment. A formal working relationship with these groups should be established for several important reasons. The most obvious need is for communication, so that the residence staff is at least aware of the goals and programs for the resident at the day activity program, and conversely, their staff is aware of the residence staff's efforts and goals. Secondly, if at all possible, house staff should try to carry over program goals of the day activity, and vice-versa. Thirdly, a sharing of information and observations about an individual gives both community residence, and day activity staff a more comprehensive and informed picture of an individual. A lack of appreciation, understanding, and communication on the part of either staff can lead to some very difficult situations.

A very clear example of this occurred in one of our houses. One individual, noted for his laziness, could never muster the energy to make his sandwiches or otherwise prepare a reasonable lunch. Instead, he would walk to the store and buy a couple of candy bars during his lunch hour. The work supervisor at the sheltered workshop questioned him about his poor eating habits. Possessing a real knack for distorting the truth, he told the supervisor in order to extricate himself from this confrontation that there was no food available for lunches at the residence. The supervisor accepted this explanation but because of a lack of communication, never discussed the situation with the community residence staff. The net effect was threefold: the supervisor thought the house staff was inadequate, if not downright malevolent; the house staff was unaware of the resident's poor eating habits; and the person himself went on eating candy bars. A phone call would have been so simple.

But other inadequacies are evident in this example, some of which are not so obvious. The indication of a lack of communication is very obvious. The willingness on the part of the supervisor to accept gross inadequacy on the part of the house staff shows a lack of respect and trust for the abilities of that staff as well as a lack of knowledge concerning the operation of the residential program. Finally, the resident himself has created a triangle between the house staff, the work supervisor, and himself and has been positively reinforced for lying. It would seem that a situation like this could have been easily avoided but things are not quite as simple.

Establishing and maintaining a good relationship with the day activity staff requires some effort. Both programs have a vested interest in the growth and welfare of the individual. Each staff has a somewhat different perspective on the abilities and needs of the individual because of the different settings in which they deal with him; therefore, each creates different goals and programs for a given person. These two sets of goals and perspectives are not always consistent and are sometimes actually contradictory, as shown in the following example.

A person, somewhat overweight and definitely food-loving, lives in a community residence. This resident is also a somewhat slow and unambitious worker in a sheltered workshop. The sheltered workshop staff, in an effort to increase his productivity, rewards the person with a bonus candy bar after every two-hour period of good production. The community residence staff, noting a weight gain, puts the person on a diet and rewards him for eating only a certain amount of food by freeing him from clean-up duties after supper. Thus, the same person is being reinforced with food for working in one situation and reinforced for not eating by not working in another. In an intellectually handicapped person, this produces confusion as well as fat.

There are some basic ways of avoiding these difficulties. The two staffs need to get to know each other well and to relate closely. They should become aware of and appreciate each other's positions as well as realize the difficulties of their various jobs. They should also become aware of the workings, constraints, goals and philosophies of each other's programs. This is a tall order in many cases, but very necessary if the people involved in the program are to live in a consistently rehabilitative environment.

Such a situation can be achieved in several ways. Making frequent visits to each other's facility and seeing what is going on is very important. Meetings to discuss programs and share information about individuals are an essential part of communicating. Having both staffs attend workshops and training programs together to share literature and methodology is important. In the end, it is a question of establishing trust and creating a good working relationship between the two staffs.

Another feature of the relationship between these staffs that presents difficulties is the fact that each has its own pecking order, but none between the two. The only way to avoid problems in this area is to clearly define roles and responsibilities with respect to each other. For example, the day activity staff is clearly responsible for and therefore makes decisions concerning vocational or educational programs. In the same way, the community residence staff is responsible for house programs such as skill training in cooking, cleaning, and independent living. There are some gray areas involved that both staffs must cover. For example, a speech impediment must be dealt with in the same way by everyone concerned if a program is to be effective. The more these roles and responsibilities can be explicated and defined, the more comfortable everyone will be, especially the residents.

A final note of caution: systems most often break down during periods of stress. These are critical situations caused by an injury, a difficult emotional period, and so forth, and these are the times when people most often stop communication with trust and appreciation for each other. Thus, since it is very easy to let a relationship lapse during less stressful periods, it becomes apparent that when a critical situation does arise, someone is even more likely to make an ill-advised or inappropriate decision. And once again its the resident who is ultimately shortchanged when this relationship breaks down.

Recreational Facilities

There are a number of opportunities available in the community for recreational activities. The most obvious one would be the YMCA, and some local Ys may give the residents free or low rates for membership. This might also be the case with Boys' Clubs and other similar organizations. They usually offer a wide variety of activities, that can be utilized for group or individual activities. However, these organizations may try to organize such things as "the retarded swim," which should be avoided. It is very important to the concept of "normalization" that the residents take part in regular courses and activities as other "normal" people do.

There are a myriad of other recreational opportunities available, such as local parks, recreation department activities, movies, theatres, a nearby university, and so forth. It does no harm to approach any group or organization to ask for anything reasonable in trying to arrange activities for residents to come in contact with other members of the community.

Volunteers

Volunteers can be useful in many areas of a community residence. They can provide special skills, allow for additional programming and set up recreational opportunities. There are, however, a few precautions worthy of mention when considering volunteers.

There are a number of sources of volunteers. An interested citizenry can be organized through the churches, Scouts, the Jay Cees, the Elks, and especially the ARC or the local Mental Health Association. These people might volunteer on their own; in other cases their volunteer services might have to be solicited. Another source of volunteers is a local college or university. Students can become involved in a variety of ways: on their own, through a student organization, or through a class or practicum situation set up by a professor. Our involvement with students has been quite successful.

Volunteers can be used in a variety of ways. They can provide a work force for doing a big job such as painting a house or cleaning a house to make it ready for residents to move in. They can also do renovation and maintenance work if they have the skills. They can provide education and training to individuals or groups, or they can act in "Big Brother" or advocacy roles that are usually one-to-one arrangements. Finally, volunteers can be used to do such day-to-day chores as taking residents to a doctor's appointment or some bookwork. There are, of course, appropriate kinds of people to approach for the different jobs to be done.

Volunteers, however, are not "free" in every respect. They need training to be effective; they require a good knowledge of the program and its goals; they need to be organized and directed so that they can be most effective in their role; and they need to be consistently involved over a period of time. Organizing and overseeing such a system is a time-consuming task. A simple example would be a house painting party. Six members of a church group can paint the house in one weekend; getting paint, brushes, scrapers, and so forth will best be done in advance by the staff if the group is to be effective in the space of a weekend.

An advocacy program would require more work on the part of the house staff. Volunteer advocates, in order to be effective, must be aware of the objectives and methods of a community residence program. Furthermore, they must be informed about the services and resources available to an individual in the community. Finally, they may require training in implementing various behavioral aspects of an individual program. All this requires time and legwork, but is necessary for a successful advocacy program. Advocates can, of course, be of the "let's go the ballgame" ilk, but this type of advocacy would be minimally effective in a rehabilitative sense. Going to a ball game is certainly a good thing to do but hopefully will be only a sidelight of an effective advocate's role.

Perhaps the major drawback of volunteers is that they become involved for short periods of time and then lose interest. Because of their volunteer status, there is little that can be done about how long they stay with the program or how they are to participate while they are involved. One method of avoiding this is to work through a college, university, or high school system to make volunteer work at the community residence part of a course. This way the people have an interest in being a part of the program for at least the duration of the academic year. Also, the staff or the course teacher can have more ability to control the students' involvement with the residence. In our own program, we have had college students providing remedial education classes, music classes, and physical education classes. These have proved to be very successful for several reasons. First, their involvement is part of their course work. Second, their roles are explicit and answer needs of the residents. Third, the roles are designed so that the students can be effective in the one, relatively short, academic year in which they are involved. Finally, although the students build friendships with the residents, they do so in a group atmosphere and the pain of leaving is not at all what it would be for the resident in a one-to-one situation. These factors and, of course, interested, bright, and dedicated students, have led to a very successful volunteer program.

Public Relations

The media and neighborhood interaction are the major contacts that the community residence program has with the community at large. As such, these are the chief means the community has of obtaining information and becoming educated about the concept of community residences. Needless to say, they can be very constructive tools if used wisely.

There are two ways in which a community residence program can be introduced to the community: the "high noon" approach and the "dark of night" approach. In the first instance, community residence staff members appear on talk shows, speak to any and all civic and fraternal organizations, get front page coverage of the house opening, or hold a reception for the mayor, the city council, and other civic leaders. The second approach is maintaining such a low profile that the community hardly realizes the home is there. Obviously, the best method will vary from location to location and lies somewhere between these two extremes.

Newspaper and radio can provide coverage of a community residence both at the opening and on a periodic basis. The newspapers usually print most local stories that are given to them, so a periodic "press release" of success is a good idea. An example might be a report of vocational or community skills advancements made by the residents: "after one year of operation, five residents are now working in competitive employment." The newspaper is also a great way of saying thank you for a donation or a volunteer's efforts. Generally, small, periodic news items keep the public aware of the program, and if the articles are positive, the community can see the program as being successful.

Involvement with civic, fraternal, and religious groups can be very important. These groups can donate materials and volunteer services for a program. If requests are going to be made from such a group, the specific service requested should be suited to the group's capabilities. A well-planned request gives the group a definite goal to talk over and, hopefully, one that can be accomplished. These groups are also a good forum for promoting increased public awareness and understanding.

It is important to consider the residents in any public relations campaign. For example, an open house might be very good from a public relations point of view, but the house is the residents' home, and they may have feelings about an invasion by civic leaders. A plea to "help the handicapped" may be heard and interpreted very differently when the listener is a "handicapped" person.

Social Services

Social services constitute a diverse group scattered throughout a number of different agencies and organizations. This group would include psychiatric services, group counseling, individual counseling, sex education, drug programs, and so forth. A large town will have various services that can fulfill these needs, and the local ARC would be a good place to begin the search. The Association may offer some of these services directly or would know the source of them. Most sheltered workshops include counseling and job placement among their rehabilitative services and sometimes have a remedial education program. A local Family Aid organization may offer needed services, and if a Mental Health Association exists, it may provide some direction. Finally, some services may be offered through the school department or through a state mental health center or other state facility.

Transportation

Another aspect of community interaction concerns getting the residents into the community, and there are many different ways of doing this. The issues involved include availability and use of transportation as well as programmatic consideration of expense and responsibility. It is important to remember that people going out of the house and into the community is desirable and that the more independently they act, the better.

There are several means of transportation available: walking, public transportation, school buses, bicycles, taxis, private vehicles, and vehicles run by the program. Walking and bicycling are the most desirable whenever possible, because the residents need to actively do something as well as exhibit a certain amount of independence. Public transportation is a good experience for residents because it puts them in contact with other people in the community; this would also apply to cabs and school buses. Finally, private vehicles, owned either by the residents themselves or by the program, should be used only when no other form of transportation is suitable. Teaching people to utilize these various modes of transportation is extremely important if independence is a goal.

The basic rule in teaching people to get around in the community seems to be simply to go with them a few times. In walking and bicycling, this means merely going with them and showing them where things are, what time things open or begin, and so forth. If bicycles are used, some basic safety rules should be taught. When considering public transportation, indicating who, when, and how much to pay is essential, as is pointing out the stops where the resident will get off. Whenever possible, the resident should be allowed to act as independently as possible, for failure is often a very valuable learning experience: The ability to take risks is basic to human dignity and is denied in almost all institutional settings. Allowing and encouraging risk-taking is very important in the "normalization" process.

Whenever a resident is going somewhere to receive professional services, there may be some consideration of a staff person going with him. A resident can very easily go to the dentist independently, after he has been shown where the office is and has shown an ability to keep appointments. However, a physical checkup at a doctor's office may require the presence of a staff person. The doctor might prescribe some medication, ask for some tests, or the resident might not understand the instructions given to him. These decisions will, of course, have to be made on an individual basis.

Many passive, formerly institutionalized people may be very hesitant to go into the community for any but the most necessary reasons. The concept of enjoying a movie, going bowling, or going to the Y may be totally alien. In fact, the whole concept of "enjoying yourself," or "relaxing," may be alien. Residents may have to learn these skills just as they learn how to ride the bus, and there are several ways to get them out into the community to begin to enjoy what it has to offer.

The most basic way of teaching these skills is to give an actual demonstration: show a resident or a group of residents where the movie page is in the newspaper and how to use it, and then go with them; show them the schedule of events at the Y, and then go to swim hour with them. This will help them learn how to use these resources and make their first attempts easier and less frightening. When they are capable, they should be encouraged to go on their own. Another valuable method is to have a resident who "knows the ropes" show another resident how to do something. One resident teaching another is a very powerful method of instruction. In sum, residents should be encouraged to go into the community, and they should be rewarded after a difficult venture has been successfully completed.

A person who has been in an institution for most or all of his life finds the community a very frightening environment. A number of successive approximations might be employed to allay some of these fears. A walk down the street with a staff member might be a good first step, then a walk around the block, and so forth, until he can go to the movies on his own and be proud of it.

Agreements can be made with a resident that encourage going into the community. An example might be: "I'll go to the movies with you tonight, if you go to the park this afternoon." Any type of reinforcement can be used to facilitate the resident going into the community, and hopefully, the end result will be that the residents in the program will use and enjoy everything the community has to offer.

5

The Families in the Community Home
Margaret T. Gerry

There are undoubtedly many occupations that push and pull at a family unit, but there are few that do so more constantly and from more directions than that of housemanager in a community residence for the retarded. Whether or not the housemanagers have children, whether or not the residents are male or female, children or adults, there is a certain amount of tension or stress that invariably accompanies work of this type. Although certain combinations of factors can compound the stress, none can completely do away with it.

The Housemanagers as a Family

One of the primary concerns of all who are interested in the durability and success of the program is the preservation of the integral family unit. It simply will not do if the housemanagers cannot function comfortably in this situation as a couple—that is, if they cannot cope with the demands of nine or ten individuals and still remain a mutually supportive unit. Not only will the effect on the marriage be detrimental, but the ease with which the residents can relate to one or both marital partners will be seriously diminished and affect, in turn, the rehabilitative atmosphere of the house. And when children are part of the family unit, the necessity of remaining a distinct and healthy aggregate is even greater: then, the responsibility of the couple is to the needs of the child as well as those of each other.

Beyond the realm of generalities, there are specific effects and pressures that should be considered. First, it has been our experience that couples interested in this job have been relatively young, and not long-married. This is not to say that couples with other characteristics would not or could not undertake this type of work, but it will limit our observations and inferences to a specific type.

When a young couple, usually married less than three or four years, takes on the role of housemanagers, the impact of an "instant family" must be considered. There will be interferences in a hitherto close and sometimes exclusive relationship that must be expected and dealt with as they arise. These range from forming separate relationships with a new and demanding group of people, some of whom will want to serve as a wedge between the

49

couple, to coping with a more rigid schedule of responsibilities and a lesser amount of alone-together time. One partner may not have considered jealousy a personal character trait until finding him/herself peevishly asking the other *why* he/she wants to stay downstairs playing cards with the guys.

This same kind of invasion of privacy may occur on a different level if a child is involved from the point of view of the child as well as of the parents. The child may react sharply to sharing his mother and father with an extended group, and the parents may at first resent the influence of the new family members on their child whose major source of social ethics has been, until now, themselves.

The ramification of this influence on the child is the source of another possible pressure, namely, the opinions of parents and in-laws concerning the effects of housemanaging. When three-year-old Mandy's vocabulary suddenly increases by a few choice words, or she calmly tells grandmother that thirty-year-old Eddy breaks windows when he is angry, or twelve-year-old Sally throws food, grandmother is going to worry. How you handle these worries is going to have a great impact on the continuing satisfaction of supportive family relationships.

One of the best ways of handling parental uneasiness is to invite the family to dinner, or have them come along on a picnic. Just about everyone enjoys eating, the atmosphere is usually more relaxed, and everyone is occupied, which are all factors that go a lot farther toward establishing understanding and acceptance than a stiff, one-hour visit in the living room. This also applies in trying to ease the relationship of the resident's family with the rest of the house and staff. A little small talk around a dinner table (provided the food is good) is great for breaking down barriers.

The Larger Family

If much of the above sounds negative, it is only because the negative aspects of any situation are the ones that will do the most damage if the couple is not prepared for them—at least in the general sense of expecting something other than a bed of roses. However, the situation of living in a community residence is basically positive. This will become apparent as we deal with individuals in the family interacting with the residents.

Generally speaking, the effect of the group home experience on the family is extremely broadening. Beginning with peripheral members, in what better way can one attack and dispel prejudices of in-laws, parents, and neighbors against retarded and disturbed people than by moving in with them and having a positive effect? In the case of the retarded, it is quite true that familiarity frees one from the generalized concept of these people as frightening or pitiable creatures, and it is an excellent remedy for dispensing with the myth of "strangeness" society has woven around this group.

The impact of a community residence on the immediate members of the housemanager family is necessarily greater than its impact on relatives and is considerably more complex. Regardless of the sex and age of the residents, the wife will be cast into a variety of roles, some of which are more readily apparent than others. And it is not only the residents who try to define the relationship and fulfill individual needs: the wife interacts for her own needs, too, and unless one is aware of these needs, the house may take a direction that is both uncomfortable and burdensome. (Of course, this is true of the husband, also, but we are concerned with female impact here, hence the use of the feminine gender.) An example will clarify this. If a woman has a strong inclination to mother—a nurturing need—she may very well find herself in the unenviable position of emptying ashtrays, doing laundry, and washing dishes for a dozen adults. This may also occur in a more subtle manner—that is, the wife becomes the house nag—since she must resort to threatening, cajoling, or reminding if anything is to be done by the residents. This situation, of course, will not only become intolerable but is diametrically opposed to the philosophy of teaching independence and responsibility. The truism that it is easier to do something yourself is treacherously applicable when dealing with institutionalized people, but yielding to the temptation will only result in the establishment of a mini-institution.

There are other aspects of mothering that warrant some attention. With adults or children, the housewife role described above is often a pitfall and not simply because of the realities of household chores. Often, people who have been institutionalized seem to adopt very rigid and clichéd ideas of role assignment. We once had a fellow who could not understand why I "The Wife" did not want to do all that was necessary in maintaining a house. It made no difference to him that she did not dirty twelve plates, sleep in twelve beds, or litter the living room with cigar butts: She was the woman; the course should have been obvious. We could theorize at length about seeing conservative attitudes as the norm in an institutional living situation where attendants are the only interpreters of outside values, of normalcy, and where defining oneself as normal is of great concern, but regardless of why people adopt such attitudes, theorizing will not banish the problem. Only constant, patient, consistent repetition of constructive roles will gradually teach the residents that meaningful normalcy is harmonious cooperation and responsible living.

When the residents are children, the foster mother relationship may be considerably more straightforward. If the children have families they see often, there may be comparison, limit-testing, or simply confusion. Constructive handling of this situation calls for clearly defining the position:

the housemanager is not a mother to these children. Although the temptation to substitute is very strong, in the long run it will be healthier if they understand this. Housemanagers do not remain housemanagers forever; it is unrealistic to expect young couples to hold such positions for more than a few years, and their leaving will be much less traumatic if the children understand from the beginning that they are teachers, models, warm and loving human beings, but not their parents. Realizing this will also make it easier to handle comparison and resentment: the residence is not a substitute family home, and therefore it is not logical to expect demands and routines to be the same. Adjustment is easier if the two living situations, community residence and home, are clearly distinct, and if that point is made, the concepts of better or worse are not relevant. Providing a healthy home environment does not mean negating an already existing home and family or replacing one that is not there, for a community residence is an entirely different experience.

The other important aspect of the wife's interaction with residents is her role as a sexual being. With male residents, it is easy to imagine the dilemma in which a woman may find herself. (Again, this is true for the husband if the residents are women.) One responsibility of housemanagers is providing models of acceptable and normal behavior, and it would be denying an important part of heterosexual interaction if husband and wife were ill at ease in showing affection, touching, and generally expressing their relationship. Naturally enough, this can lead to attempts by the residents to enjoy the same kind of interaction, and if the wife is the only available female, that means jealousy, resentment, and a generally unhealthy atmosphere. When we first became housemanagers, one of the younger residents would follow me around and talk for as long as I would respond. We encouraged this because he was usually taciturn, unfriendly, and awkward, and we thought it would help him acquire the skills to begin interacting with others. What actually happened was that he gradually started leaving the room when my husband came in or tried to instigate verbal or physical encounters with him. When it became obvious to him that he was not going to separate us, I became as much a target for his frustration and anger as my husband, and it even extended to our daughter. Eventually, the only member of the family to whom he did not react violently was our dog, and he would play with her only if he thought we were elsewhere.

Another eye-opener occurred at a housemeeting when the residents and our consulting psychologist were discussing women and sexual relationships. One resident unhesitatingly said that one of the things that bothered him about living in the house was that my husband always had first chance with me. That he was my husband apparently was not a sufficient explanation of the situation for this resident. These kinds of incidents only develop into full-scale problems if they are not dealt with decisively. It is not enough to rely on the resident's understanding of the terms of social conventions like marriage, and attitudes like the above require explicit verbal clarification. One more thing to remember is that it is flattering to be the sole sexual object of any group, but subtle or unconscious encouragement in a community residence situation is very harmful to both the residents and the spouse, whether husband or wife.

To be effective, both partners must develop ways of showing the residents what a man/woman relationship means and how it can develop, and at the same time minimize or sidestep altogether being a potential in the sexual field. It should be obvious that the most successful way of achieving this is to encourage going out and doing things that will lead to satisfying heterosexual experiences. If a coed community residence is not possible, the next best thing is locating residences for men and women within easy visiting distance.

We have been speaking, for the most part, of the attitudes and roles of the husband and wife as interchangeable, depending on the sex of the residents, but just as residents will try to define women in conventional ways, men are also subject to stereotyping, and as with any stereotype, it can cause frustration to both partners if this situation is not recognized. Residents in institutions see men in a variety of authoritarian positions—from doctor to attendant. If experience has taught them that comfortable survival depends on submission and/or manipulation, that is the attitude with which they will approach the male housemanager. This can result in behaviors that range from destructiveness ("I need to be controlled") to total passivity ("I am helpless"). Both of these patterns will interfere with the resident adapting to normal community living, and such patterns should be replaced with healthier, more responsible attitudes. This is accomplished by refusing to become the authority or by reacting to destructiveness in unexpected ways. If a resident misses the bus for work and returns home with a what-do-I-do-now look, he cannot be allowed to stay home nor should he be taken to work. The responsibility should be put back where it belongs by asking him how he intends to get there (the implication being that staying home is not an alternative). Suggestions are fine, but arbitrary solutions will never teach someone to initiate responses to situations. In a similar way, falling into the trap of conventional punishment for destructive behavior should be avoided. We had a fellow who embodied manipulation. He would act aggressively or destructively to gain attention or avoid doing something he did not want to do and then run away to escape the consequences. He definitely did not want to be left alone, and he also did not want to have to make decisions. He wanted someone else to shoulder the responsibility of making him do what had to be done and of rescuing him when he ran away. At the institution, all his demands were met: he was punished by others and made to do things; he was chased and brought back when he ran away; and consequently, he was universally admired by other residents. In other words, he was always the center of attention.

When he began to break windows and tear his clothes to protest his responsibilities at the community residence, we fortuitously hit upon the right response. No one yelled at him or locked him up. Instead, he was told he would have to pay for new clothes and new windows, and that whenever he purposely broke something or left work, he would not be allowed in the house for two hours. Far from being chased when he ran away, he was confronted with the other extreme of being put out into the world if he could not act responsibly in his present living situation. He tested this to the limit, and things finally climaxed on the day he was barred from the house for six successive two-hour periods. After that, he never broke another window and did everything expected of him as a contributing member of the house.

It is never only the wife who is cast in the mother role or the husband as the figure of authority; more often, aspects of both roles are combined. And just as it is important to clarify the sexual interaction of husband and wife with the residents, it is also necessary to help the residents achieve an understanding of the place of authority, submission, initiative, and compassion in any lifestyle. Then, when they are ready for more independent living, each will have sufficient social knowledge to adapt to people and situations with a greater amount of success and ease, whether it involves dealing with a new landlord or finding another job.

The third member of the housemanaging family may not exist in many cases, and there are some instances where this should be the rule. In a house for adults, children not only seem to fit in, but to belong. There is little of the normal rhythm of life in an institution, but that does not lessen the desire for it. Most residents have had little daily contact with children and are delighted at the chance to mother, father, aunt, or uncle someone on a continuing basis. There are exceptions, of course, but for the most part, a child can be a great addition as long as some of the usual family dynamics, such as sibling rivalry, spoiling, and playing one against the other, are kept in mind. Even with adults (and remember, institutionalized adults have always been treated like children), demands for attention will at some point compete with the same demands from the child, and the result will be the same hurt feelings that would surface in any family group. Residents may also try to assume parenting responsibilities of correcting, verbally and physically. Depending on the judgment of the resident as well as his motive (jealousy or real concern), this may or may not be allowable. In any event, the interaction of resident and child usually seems to be mutually advantageous. The child is exposed to a larger number of people with whom he can develop relationships, which thus lessens the intensity of the parent/only child experience on both sides; he becomes much more tolerant and accepting of people with a wide range of abilities and personalities; and he becomes the object of a great deal of healthy, extra-family affection. The resident, on the other hand, can see on-the-spot example of childishness that can be used to encourage responsibility and more adult behaviors. In addition, he has someone who will both give and receive affection and who is apt to be spontaneous and forthright in his reactions to different kinds of behavior: children seem to have a sense that intuitively discriminates between the real and the spurious in the areas of interest and affection.

The one type of community residence that does not appear to benefit from the presence of a child is the one for other children. This is certainly not to be construed as an impossible situation, but as far as our experience goes, it is the case more often than not and for the obvious reasons. Regardless of how generous the parents are with their affection or how indiscriminatory their behavior is to all the children in the residence, it is still a fact that their child is their own, that he will accompany them on vacation, and that he will go with them when they leave. Every child has a need for a relationship that is solid; no amount of affection or explanation will be sufficient to fill that need, and every child will recognize the situation for what it is regardless of how mature he may seem. Since children in a community residence are already subject to a myriad of demands and adjustments, it seems more logical to try to eliminate another major source of stress by hiring housemanagers without children of their own. This is also more sensible from the housemanagers' point of view: in ways, working in a residence for children is much more taxing than working with adults, both because of the energy levels necessary and the responsibility involved. Situations in which the number of children is very small may be different, but a house with six or eight children is extremely demanding.

There is one additional family member to be considered: cat, dog, guinea pig, rabbit—in short, the house pet. Although it may sound like just one more creature to worry about and care for, the benefits make it almost essential. In our opinion, the best type is a medium-sized, gentle, overly affectionate animal who considers himself a lap dog. There is nothing that makes a house more instantly homey than a dog who wags his tail when you come in, begs for food, and is always ready for a walk. For adult residents, a pet is something that is totally undemanding. It will greet them with joy whether or not they did everything they were supposed to do during the day, and it will be good company regardless of moods. For children, a pet will almost always want to play, and something soft and warm and furry can be very soothing. We have seen both children and adults who related to people very minimally, but who were able to express affection and warmth to a dog, and that seems a very good starting point for coaxing someone out of withdrawal into more spontaneous and giving relationships.

Space in the Community Home

Although the interaction of the family and the residents is the prime factor in defining the tenor of the home, the physical aspect of the house has an important part. Much research has been done on the contributions of size, color, and arrangement of rooms to the general well-being of the people inhabiting them, and it is a mistake to think that the crowded, communal conditions of many institutions leave the residents without the normal re-actions of any individual to his surroundings. Indeed, the rehabilitative effect of a little normal privacy and the use of non-institutional furnishings and colors is enormous. The first reactions of a previously institutionalized person may be discouraging—there is little decorative self-expression, and maintaining the condition of what might be considered a beautiful bed-room just is not that important. However, as the resident becomes aware that what is in his room is personally his, that his bedspread and curtains are not interchangeable with Joe's down the hall, he is apt to buy some others—to be personally responsible for the choice. No matter how they clash with the color of the room or how atrocious the pattern, this is an important step toward autonomous thinking and the development of a definite identity that should definitely be encouraged. The acquisition of personal possessions may be considered trivial or materialistic, but it is nevertheless an immeasurably valuable aid in the deinstitutionalization of a personality and is one of the first moves toward independence and the acceptance of responsibility.

The number of rooms necessary in a community residence has been discussed elsewhere, but it is important to emphasize the need for privacy, and this means more than having only one or two people in one bedroom. A house with only a living room, dining room, and kitchen as common rooms does not have enough living space. There are many times when residents want to do something other than watch television with five or six others—that is, talking privately with a friend, making a table or a bird-house, or simply sitting quietly in front of the fire. Bedrooms do not begin to fill all these needs, especially when they are shared. Most of our houses have at least one extra room on the first floor in addition to a cellar that can be used as a workshop and a porch that is invariably popular.

Having extra rooms does not imply a higher furniture budget if you keep in mind that new, expensive furniture is definitely not necessary for creating a happy home. Comfortable, resilient, second-hand pieces are not only infinitely more sittable, they are also easily acquired. Most parents (housemanagers' or residents') will be flattered and pleased if they are asked to contribute something from home. As with the family dinner, helping out is an instant ice-breaker.

Much more important than the quality of the furniture is the color of the rooms and the degree of clutter. If a room looks cheerful, clean, and reasonably tidy, there is more of an impetus to keep it that way than if it never looks good no matter what is done to it. However, in the beginning this may not be enough. In an institution, the resident is never ultimately responsible. Although many institutions have independent living programs in which self care is stressed, these programs still exist in and are part of the institution—the great caretaker. And when pre-independent living programs do not exist—when ward life is the situation immediately preceding the community residence—not only is there nothing to be responsible for, but the very concept of a home is quite foreign. All of this is leading up to the fact that, for a while, some people are simply not going to see dirt, dust, old newspapers, or overflowing ashtrays. If you have the slightest tendency toward compulsive housekeeping, you are going to suffer, for it is extremely important that housework be evenly divided among the residents, and that each be held responsible for an assigned job.

Duties in the Community Home

There is much substance to the belief that people appreciate the value of something they do themselves or are responsible for getting done, and this is demonstrably true in the care and upkeep of a house. If the residents help with cleaning and refurbishing, things will stay in good condition longer. It may be a trying experience to teach someone to paint a wall or clean a rug, but it means he will know how to do it in the future, and he will take a personal interest in its treatment by others. This is true for every job, from mowing the lawn to cleaning the bathroom, and the key to success is the housemanager's ability to teach and direct without resorting to doing it himself.

The houses with which we are involved are maintained on a rotating job system. A list of household responsibilities is prepared, and each resident chooses one (assignment is sometimes necessary). Then, for a given period of time, that job is his responsibility: he is the one to whom all complaints concerning it are directed, and he is held accountable. This system works well for a number of reasons. Each resident has a clearly defined task that he can do when and how he likes, providing it is done well and as often as necessary. This allows the freedom of deciding how to go about something, and the reward of solving a problem. Secondly, each resident has the opportunity to learn all aspects of the work involved in independent living without being overwhelmed by total responsibility before he can handle it. Thirdly, the concept of cooperation is established as well as the accompanying awareness of accountability for the comfort of others. Finally, the drudgery of repetitive housework is avoided; no one keeps the same job forever.

The one thing you can be sure of in a community residence is that regardless of its value, a system like this never runs smoothly, and therefore at least a few problems can be expected. Almost invariably, there is one person in the group who is extremely conscientious. He does his job perfectly from the beginning and in addition to being more than willing to do whatever else needs to be done, he can usually do it better than the person whose responsibility it is. The temptation here is to rely on the good nature and competence of such a person for the weary housemanager will feel mortally tired of showing everyone else for the eighteenth time how to do their jobs right. Although giving in may do wonders for the housemanager's peace of mind, it will contribute nothing to the ultimate success of the home.

Another area of dissension will be the definition of a job well done. Usually, the housemanagers are the only ones to criticize any aspect of housekeeping: no one else seems to notice greasy dishes, sticky floors, or foot-high grass. However, sanity, the good feelings of the residents, and the continued approval of the board of health can depend on emphasizing good work skills continuously through gentle, supportive, non-destructive indication of a job less than well done. Developing this knack may prove elusive for some housemanagers, but it is important because the physical aspects of the house (cleanliness, order, and so forth) are the most visible to neighbors and other community people interested in its impact on their town. While it may be unfair, the immediate (sometimes lasting) impressions are often based on the presence or absence of dirt and dust, and these impressions are of consequence in establishing community support and acceptance.

One area of housekeeping remains to be covered, and this is definitely a case of last, but not least. Food is of great interest to every member of the community residence. Type, purchase, and preparation are a few of the considerations involved. When the population is mainly formerly institutionalized, there are likely to be problems from the outset. Not only will the majority of residents lack most cooking skills, they will also often have food-related health problems (poor nutrition, obesity, bad teeth, to name but a few) and peculiar notions of what constitutes a balanced diet. We know a resident who still prefers six or seven slices of bread and butter to any kind of dinner. Some poor eating habits can never be changed, but others will often respond readily to a strong dose of good cooking and appetizing foods.

For a while, good cooking may not exist, unless the housemanagers do it themselves. This is fine if it is incorporated into teaching a resident, for there is no better incentive for learning to cook than eating a delicious concoction he helped prepare. We have found that all aspects of food preparation are of interest to most residents. Seeing the inside of a supermarket is a new experience for many of these people, and they greatly enjoy shopping. Also, there is immediate gratification in cooking a good meal: verbally from the other residents and sensually from the tastebuds.

Our system of food preparation is basically very simple. Everyone is responsible for his own breakfast and lunch, and for cooking dinner (in pairs) for everyone one night a week. In the beginning, we asked for a list of favorite foods from each person and then helped him plan and cook a meal including these foods (the simpler, the better, at first). After the rudiments of cooking were mastered, we assigned two residents for each weekday to be responsible for choosing and cooking dinner. We had compiled a list of possibilities with all ingredients noted. Each pair then had to choose a meal from this list and write their selection on the menu board. Ideally, each pair would be responsible for buying whatever was necessary, but since this was impractical, only a few residents would usually accompany the housemanagers to the grocery store to help with all food purchases for the week. We discovered that this system would work remarkably well for a few weeks—that is, interesting and fairly well-prepared meals were served by the residents. Then, decline would set in. Joe would decide to cook hotdogs and beans for the third week in a row, and residents would start eating out. This was easily remedied by making a demand at the weekly housemeeting for a week's menu of meals that nobody had ever prepared before. This plan required help in interpreting the cook book and following directions and meant supervising the cooking, but it was well worth it. Dinner was varied and good once again, and everyone perked up. We heaped praise on worthy efforts, even if the results left a little to be desired, and the chef would blush with pride. A second Julia Child may never emerge from a community residence, but healthier and happier residents (and staff) certainly will. Learning the elements of good nutrition and the basics of where and what to buy and how to incorporate this knowledge into a few simple, but good meals, is invaluable to everyone, regardless of goals. If a resident is heading toward independent living, this experience is essential.

Leaving the Community Residence

It has been mentioned before that it would be highly unlikely for any couple to remain for a long period as managers of a community residence.

It is an invaluable living and learning experience, but it requires constant attention and involvement, and the wear involved is greater than any two week vacation can compensate for. If a child is part of the family, or if more children are planned, time and space will become factors for consideration and will lead, eventually, to leaving.

Leaving is always difficult for the residents if the housemanagers have been competent and effective in the slightest degree, for the relationship has been close and dependent, even if independence has been stressed as a goal. When the departure is made by the first housemanagers the residents have experienced, the separation can be very traumatic. However, there are a number of ways of lessening the intensity of the situation. It will help if the housemanagers are always honest about their position in the house—that is, they are not parents or guardians, but friends and teachers. At some point during their tenure as housemanagers, the question of permanence is likely to arise. Again, honest answers about the position being a job and emphasis on the fact that people often change jobs can also be helpful, particularly if the housemanagers plan to stay in the area and can soften that explanation by appending, "But we will still see you and come over for dinner." The most concrete way of easing the transition is to allow time for the new housemanagers to become familiar with everyone and everything before the outgoing housemanagers leave. This requires planning a few months in advance to provide time for hiring replacements, allowing for their gradual entrance into the program, and giving the residents opportunity to accustom themselves to the idea. It is extremely important to avoid the setback and loss of trust that would result from a hasty exit.

As former housemanagers, we have had a very positive experience after leaving the community residence, because we have remained not only in the same town, but just a few streets away from the residence. This has made possible a continuity of feeling and interaction for all concerned and has made it easier for the residents to understand what a changing relationship entails in a positive, rather than threatening way.

6

Selection and Training of Housemanagers
Joel S. Bergman

Recruitment of Housemanagers

The effectiveness of the housemanagers in a community home is viewed as one of the most important aspects of running a successful community home. It is thought that the intelligence, personality characteristics, and social skills of housemanagers seem to influence and perhaps determine the atmosphere of the community home and that this atmosphere should foster a resident's physical, intellectual, and emotional growth. Consequently, the selection of housemanagers should be performed with the utmost of thought and care.

The director of Community Homes and the present author, who is the consulting psychologist to the program, were responsible for the recruitment and hiring of housemanagers for four adult community homes. One of the first problems we encountered in hiring the housemanagers was the vagueness with which we viewed the characteristics of an ideal housemanager. What would be the characteristics of ideal or even effective housemanagers? If such people existed, would they be interested in considering the job, and would they accept the job when the offer was made? Are certain characteristics of housemanager candidates considered more important than others, and would there be certain characteristics of housemanagers that would interfere with a community home program?

We obviously had no answers to any of these questions, since we had no previous experience in this area, and little research data had been reported in the literature to assist us in this task. We did try to express to each other in concrete terms those characteristics we believed would facilitate effectiveness, and found considerable consensus. Both of us felt that if we had our druthers, the housemanagers would be intelligent (not only intelligent, but also smart about people), emotionally mature, motivated to do a good job, optimistic, flexible; interested in people and working in the helping professions; and interesting and likable, since we had to work with whomever we hired.

Rather than keeping all these characteristics in mind and hiring only those people who came closest to the ideal housemanager, we agreed to take a more practical approach and interview as many people as possible (if that's practical) to see what special skills and characteristics a variety of candidates could contribute to the job.

Recruitment of Housemanagers

A job description was written to clarify to housemanager candidates the nature of the responsibilities and duties involved in the position. This job description, which can be seen in Appendix A, also clarified in our own minds what was expected of the housemanager.

We discovered an additional advantage of having a written job description in that it serves as an informal contract between the housemanagers and their employer. When housemanagers agree to take the position after seeing a written job description, they are responsible to fulfill the duties and responsibilities included therein. On the other hand, the job description protects the housemanagers from having to perform duties or for being responsible for matters that are *not* expressed in the job description.

Once the job description was constructed, a newspaper advertisement was written and placed for two week periods in various newspapers. The advertisement, which simply stated that a couple was wanted to act as housemanagers in a home for formerly institutionalized, mentally handicapped adults, was placed in local newspapers in large cities (population over 100,000) within a one hundred mile radius. It was assumed that people interested in the job would be willing to travel this distance to interview for the job, and this assumption turned out to be correct.

In addition to the newspaper advertisements, a job description was placed on bulletin boards in departments of psychology, education, and special education at local colleges and universities. We also "passed the word" on to colleagues, other professionals, and friends to let them know we were interested in hiring housemanagers to work in a community home for the retarded.

The interviewing procedures began once candidates for the job began contacting the director. When candidates phoned for appointments for interviews, the job was briefly described with respect to the population of people they would be working with, the live-in situation, duties and responsibilities, and salary. At this particular point, some candidates indicated that they were not interested in the job.

When candidates remained interested in the position after this brief description, they were given appointments for their interviews with the director and were also asked to bring résumés. At the first interview, the director described the housemanager position in greater detail, answered questions, and gave the prospective housemanagers tours of both the sheltered workshop and some of the established community homes. Housemanager candidates had opportunities to talk to housemanagers and to the residents of some of these homes.

If the first interview proceeded successfully, candidates were asked whether they would be willing to complete a pencil-and-paper personality inventory called the *Minnesota Multiphasic Personality Inventory* (MMPI) (Hathaway and McKinley 1943). They were told that the MMPI was being given to all candidates who were seriously considering the job in order to collect some research data on the types of people interested in such a job as well as those who are successful in this kind of work. It should be noted, parenthetically, that the descriptive data on housemanagers to be reported in this chapter are limited to those candidates who reached the second interview level of the selection process. This second interview level included candidates who remained interested after the first interview was completed and in whom the director was interested after the first interview.

The majority of candidates who did reach the second interview level did so on their own accord. After receiving more information about the position during the first interview, some people decided that they were not interested; a few people did not reach the second interview level because the director was not interested in hiring them. Some of the reasons for not considering these candidates included their not being too bright; their seeking the job to obtain U.S. citizenship; their being fired from a similar job; their having no particular strengths or skills for the job; and their wanting to hold down a second job in addition to the housemanager position. Thus, before the second interview, a considerable degree of selection occurred, based upon additional information obtained by both the candidate and by the director.

The second interview was held usually a week after the first interview and included the director, the present author, and the candidates—usually a married couple. If the couple had a child, the entire family was invited to this interview. By this time, the present author had received the résumé and completed MMPI, which had been scored and interpreted prior to the interview.

After interviewing a few couples, the MMPI was included as a standard part of the selection process. The test was administered for a few reasons. First, it was considered valuable to start collecting data on candidates who are interested in a housemanager type of position. The MMPI scores could be helpful in developing hypotheses about the personality characteristics of people interested in such positions. Second, with a large number of MMPI profiles, a research program could be initiated to examine the MMPI characteristic of successful and of unsuccessful housemanagers.

The MMPI was also administered to contribute additional information to the selection process. The present author has employed the MMPI in both clinical and research settings and has found the instrument to be one of the more valid and reliable psychological tests in detecting *severe* emotional disturbance in subjects. The MMPI was used with the assumption that the test could accurately assess severe emotional disturbances in subjects; it was also assumed that severe disturbances in housemanagers would interfere with their doing an adequate job. The MMPI was not used as an initial screening device nor as a major source of information in the selection procedure. It simply was considered one of many sources of information.

The second interview provided another opportunity for the candidates to ask questions about the position. This meeting also provided opportunities to learn more about the couple and to evaluate further how they would be suited to the role of housemanagers. Since the present author is also interested in family therapy, the couples were asked to describe and comment on their own families of origin as well as on their own marriage situations. Describing families of origin provided some information about the candidates themselves, their intelligence, flexibility, level of psychological sophistication, sensitivities to others, and how they might handle the "parenting" role in a community home. Commenting on their marriage provided similar information as well as clues as to how well and functional the marriages seemed to be. We felt it was necessary to select people whose marriage seemed gratifying and functional since we did not want to introduce the adverse effects of a strained marriage to some of the stressful aspects associated with being housemanagers nor did we want to introduce such a marriage into a community home. We also wanted to provide good models of a working marriage to our residents and to approximate a rewarding family-type of environment for the community home.

After the second interview, the director and the present author discussed the candidates and offered the couple the job when there was consensus between the two of us. When we were still interested in the couple, but seemed hesitant, or not completely sure about certain matters, we arranged to see the individuals for a third interview. This interview took place in the couple's home when that was convenient. The third interview was probably the most comfortable for the candidates, since they had already talked with us during two previous interviews, and because they were in their own homes. In this more comfortable situation, we were able to see the couple more as people rather than as interviewees, which gave us a more realistic impression of their suitability for the position.

In an egalitarian spirit, we asked a few of the candidates to spend some time in an informal interview with residents of the community home where they might be working. Our thought was that since residents had more contact and experience with housemanagers than we did and had to live under the supervision of these people, perhaps the residents' point of view would be an additional source of information to consider in hiring housemanagers. We therefore invited some candidates to have dinner in one of the community homes and spend some time chatting with the residents.

The director and the present author then interviewed the residents about their impressions of the housemanager candidates. In general, the residents enjoyed having the opportunity to participate in the selection process. Unfortunately, the residents' judgments were not very discriminating, as the usual response was that the candidates were "O.K." Other reasons given by the residents for hiring the candidates included remarks about their having a "cute baby" or the female housemanager having a "good build."

In general, the selection of effective housemanagers is a very difficult yet important task. There are many unanswered questions and variables involved in deciding on which characteristics facilitate being an effective housemanager. As we continue to collect data and develop more experience in hiring housemanager couples, perhaps there will be less guesswork involved with this task in the future.

Some features of our selection process are more useful than others in hiring effective managers. Interviewing the candidates two or three times does provide a more accurate picture of the candidates because they have become more comfortable with the interview situation and the interviewers. The use of the MMPI to select out very disturbed candidates is also helpful. In the final analysis, however, a good deal of sensitivity and intuition on the interviewers' part must be relied upon until more research findings become available.

Characteristics of Housemanagers

Table 6–1 provides some demographic information about our current and past housemanagers. This information is provided to give the reader some idea of the variety of people who are interested in, accept, and function successfully in housemanager positions. There were no differences found for the information listed in the table between people we hired and people who were not hired, nor is there necessarily any relationship between the information listed in the table and hiring an individual or that individual later becoming a successful housemanager. More information and interviewing of many more candidates is necessary in order to do research on predicting successful housemanagers.

As can be seen in Table 6–1, our housemanagers are in their twenties and come from a variety of socioeconomic and religious backgrounds. Most have a bachelor's degree in areas unrelated to special education or retardation, and while a few have graduate degrees, some have not completed college. There is considerable variation in the length of the housemanager couples' marriages with the range being from six months to nine

Table 6-1
Demographic Information on Housemanagers [a]

Couple	Sex	Age	Father's or Mother's Highest Income (M)	Religion	Education	Major	Years Married	No. of Children	Age of Child	Past experience working with retarded people	Previous Work Experience	Length of Time Served as Housemanager	Way in Which Housemanagers Learned about Position
1	M	24	12	Episcopal	BA	Phil.	3	1	2	no	Part-Time Work	18 Mos.	Neighbor
1	F	24	15	R. Cathol.	MA	Bio.	3	1	2	no	Res. Ass't.	18 Mos.	Neighbor
2	M	29	15	Protestant	MS	Rehab.	9	1	2½	yes	Rehab. MR	18 Mos.	Approached by the Director
2	F	27	27	Protestant	BS	El.Ed.	9	1	2½	yes	Social Worker	18 Mos.	
3	M	27	19	R. Cathol.	3 yr.		3½	1	2½	no	Construction Writer, Sect.	Presently Employed	Friend
3	F	27	10	Episcopal	BA	Rus.His.	3½	1	2½	yes	Summer Work	Presently Employed	
4	M	22	8	Greek Orth.	BA	Am.His.	2	0	0	no	Summer Work	Presently Employed	Newspaper Ad
4	F	22	70	Jewish	BA	Eng.	2	0	0	no	Teacher	Presently Employed	
5	M	27	9	Jewish	MA	Am.His.	1	0	0	no	Sp.Ed.	Presently Employed	Professional Word-Passing
5	F	27	20	Jewish	MA	Sp.Ed.	1	0	0	yes	Aid, Day Care	Presently Employed	
6	M	23	45	Jewish	3 yr.	Sp.Ed.	½	0	0	yes	Counselor, MR	Presently Employed	Dept.Sp.Ed.
6	F	23	11	Jewish	2 yr.	Sp.Ed.	½	0	0	yes	Trainer, Beh.Mod.	Presently Employed	
7	M	23	10	Bahai	3 yr.	Sp.Ed.	1	0	0	yes	Teacher	Presently Employed	Dept.Sp.Ed.
7	F	25	10	Bahai	BS	Chem.	1	0	0	no	Counselor, MR	Presently Employed	
8	M	24	10	Episcopal	3 yr.	Eng.Lit	1	0	0	yes	Counselor, MR	Presently Employed	Through Sister, Also a Housemanager
8	F	24	25	Episcopal	2 yr.		1	0	0	yes	Counselor, MR	Presently Employed	

[a] At the time hired.

years. Interestingly, all the couples with a child began their positions when the child was two or two-and-a-half years old.

A little over half of the housemanagers have had prior work experiences with retarded people. These previous experiences included working as a trainer, aid, or counselor in state schools, summer camps for the retarded, rehabilitation centers, or special education classes. However, since many of our exceptional houseparents have not had prior work experience with retarded people, related previous work experience with retarded people should not be considered an important criterion for hiring housemanagers. More importantly, since most of our housemanagers have had successful past experience in jobs unrelated to working with retarded people, this successful work experience should be used as a criterion for selecting them. It is presently thought that a good history in any type of work infers that the housemanager candidate has certain characteristics that facilitates his performance as a housemanager. These qualities include showing responsibility, commitment, good judgment, and having the necessary social skills to relate well to superiors and fellow workers.

Table 6–1 also suggests, from our very limited sample, that the average length of time that couples remain in housemanager jobs is 18 months. This presents certain problems as well as some advantages, both of which will be discussed later in this chapter. Finally, it appears that our housemanagers learned about the job opening from indirect or informal sources rather than from more formal sources such as newspaper advertisements.

The information about our housemanagers that has been presented thus far does not provide any data on the specific characteristics of housemanager candidates that will facilitate or detract from their being successful housemanagers. Unfortunately, our research program characterizing housemanagers has just started, and we have neither seen a sufficient number of candidates nor had the time to evaluate the effectiveness of our present housemanagers to be able to answer some of the important questions about hiring effective housemanagers. However, some recommendations can be made for prospective employers but it should be kept in mind that these are based upon limited experiences and considerable speculation.

First of all, it is important to make the job opening known to as many people as possible and in as many ways possible. "Spreading the word" effectively determines, in part, the quality of the candidates who will be interviewed. The interviews should be conducted with as many couples as time and energy permit. There is no ideal couple, and it is advantageous to have choices in weighing one set of strengths in one couple with a different set of strengths in a different couple.

A married couple serving as housemanagers appears to have certain advantages over an unmarried couple or two men or two women serving in this role. Although this author is well aware of relationships where an unmarried couple might have a more meaningful and effective relationship than a married couple, when all other things are considered equal, there are more advantages in having a married couple. Commitment to each other, differences in roles, and the division of labor all contribute to potential modeling and learning opportunities for the residents. The married housemanagers might also be able to more comfortably express the "mothering" and "fathering" roles that typically occur in a family setting, and these different roles might be expressed less often with unmarried couples or with two men or two women serving as housemanagers. In addition, although very speculative, this author is increasingly seeing the advantages in hiring housemanagers who already have a child (see Chapter 5). Once again, when all other factors are equal, a couple married a few years (three or more) seems preferable to a recently married couple. There are many problems newly married couples must deal with, and working out these problems might reduce the necessary time and energy that should be devoted to the function of housemanaging.

A history of successful work experiences in jobs related or unrelated to working with retarded people is another good indicator of a potentially successful housemanager for the reasons given earlier in this chapter. Here, successful work experience refers to being able to remain in one particular job for over a year and leaving a particular job for a more interesting or rewarding position. Obviously, one cannot and should not use this criterion with people who have not had opportunities to develop job experiences. This would apply, for example, to recently graduated college students whose work experiences are usually limited to part-time summer employment.

The use of the MMPI in the selection of housemanagers and in characterizing our housemanagers deserves some discussion. We have collected around 30 MMPI profiles from housemanager candidates and will continue to do so eventually to obtain sufficiently reliable data to discuss the characteristics of successful and unsuccessful housemanagers. We do have some preliminary findings about the use of the MMPI in the selection procedure and the MMPI profile characteristics of our housemanagers.

During the selection process, we have used the results of the MMPI in one or two cases to discontinue our selection procedure and interviewing sequence. Two housemanager candidates were not further considered for the position because the MMPI profile suggested that both of these individuals were seriously disturbed. The MMPI can accurately detect severe disturbances in individuals 80 percent of the time (Marks and Sines 1969), and we could not gamble with the 20 percent chance that these particular results were wrong.

The MMPI findings on our past and present housemanagers are interesting and in some ways unexpected until one looks at the housemanagers in contrast to more conventional jobs. The profile for all the female housemanagers fall well within the normal range of scores (Gilberstadt and Duker 1965). Scores for the male housemanagers are much more deviant, in a statistical sense, from the general population. The deviancy often is found on an MMPI scale that measures family discord, rebelliousness, and nonconventional ideas or values and on a scale that measures conventional masculine and feminine ideas and values. Deviancy on these two scales for males makes sense when one looks closely at the nature of the male house-manager's job since it deviates considerably from the more conventional jobs or professions associated with the male role. It will be interesting to continue collecting MMPI profiles on housemanager candidates to eventually obtain more reliable information about the MMPI characteristics of these people.

Replacing Housemanagers

The procedures involved in the recruitment and selection of housemanagers should be viewed as a continuous, ongoing function in maintaining a community home program. When the average length of stay of a housemanager couple in a community home is 18 months, which has been the case in our program, then sufficient planning and time must be devoted to replacing the departing housemanagers with a new couple. Approximately six weeks should be sufficient time for the recruitment and selection of new house-managers.

There are some advantages and disadvantages associated with house-managers leaving a community home and being replaced with new people. Some of the residents become quite attached to the housemanagers and are visibly upset when housemanagers decide to leave. However, certain steps can be taken to reduce the disruption created by the departure. Departing housemanagers should inform the program director and the residents of their plans to leave at least two months in advance. Considerable discussion during the subsequent weekly house meeting should be focused on giving the residents opportunities to express their feelings about the departing housemanagers and to give the housemanagers opportunities to share their feelings about leaving the residents. The program director and/or the psychological consultant should attend these meetings to give the residents a sense of the stability and continuity of the program and to show the residents that things will be the same even though there will eventually be some changes when the new housemanagers arrive.

Once the housemanagers give their two-month notice, the recruitment and selection process should vigorously begin with the expectation of being able to hire a new couple within a six-week period of time. When new housemanagers are hired within this period of time, the remaining two-week period becomes an important overlapping transition period. During this period, the new housemanagers should spend considerable time with the departing housemanagers to learn about such important matters as house routines, procedures, and behavioral programs for each resident. The transitional period also gives the new housemanagers opportunities to spend time with the residents, attend the weekly group meetings, have dinner with the residents, and generally get to know the residents for a two-week period before the former housemanagers leave. Developing rapport with the residents makes the transition and break from the former housemanagers less abrupt for the residents; it also gives the new housemanagers a more comfortable and less abrupt introduction to their new job.

Although the disadvantages outweigh the advantages when there is a changeover in housemanagers, some learning opportunities do occur for the community home residents. First, the residents have the opportunity to develop a close relationship with a new pair of housemanagers or with a new family when the housemanagers have a child. Second, the residents learn to cope with the experience of parting with people they care about and to accept that they were not responsible for the departure. One could ask "Are these learning experiences necessary?"—particularly for people who have, in effect, been abandoned by their own parents. Since no individual is protected from the experiences of separation from or loss of a loved one and consistent with the principle of normalization (Nirje 1969), our residents should indeed have the same learning and experiential opportunities as everyone else.

The adjustment to new housemanagers is probably more difficult for children in community homes to make than is the adjustment for adults. We are hopeful that the 18-month period of employment of our two former housemanager couples is not a consistent pattern and that subsequently hired housemanagers will decide to remain for longer periods of time. Another consideration in hiring housemanagers might therefore be the period of time that a couple plans to stay in a particular area or community. A couple with a child or children or a couple with one partner enrolled in a doctoral program at a university may have more of an incentive to remain in a community for a longer period of time than would a couple with less responsibilities or commitments.

Training of Housemanagers

The training of our housemanagers was greatly facilitated by their young ages, which in our program ranged from 22 to 29 years. Certain characteristics associated with young people, such as their idealism, enthusiasm, and optimism, creates an atmosphere in a community home that is therapeutic.

When housemanagers have high expectations for their residents, these expectations are perceived by the residents and in many instances lead to changes in their behavior. Obversely, when managers have low or no expectations for their residents, the resident's behavior will probably not go beyond these expectations.

In addition to the housemanager's youthfulness, another factor that facilitated their training was, paradoxically, their lack of experience as housemanagers or working in a community home. This author has found that teaching staff to unlearn and relearn ways of viewing behavior is a much more difficult task than teaching people concepts for the first time. We therefore did not have to spend much time eliminating attitudes and approaches found in some of the "seasoned" and "experienced" staff who work in institutions and schools for the retarded. Some of the attitudes that we did *not* have to deal with include such misconceptions as I.Q. measures intelligence; people with low I.Q.s can't be expected to do much; brain damage is irreversible, therefore you cannot expect these people to change or even to learn; specific treatment, as in medical model notions, is related to specific diagnoses; and brain damage explains behavior. The majority of our housemanagers held the view that the behavior of their residents could be changed by learning, education, and rehabilitation, rather than by diagnosis, treatment, or use of drugs. In an unexpected way, we found some of the community home assistants to be oriented more towards diagnostic terminology, drug treatment, and other medical model approaches than our housemanagers. These assistants will be discussed in greater detail later in this chapter.

Newly hired housemanagers have to quickly become familiar with the various state and local medical, educational, and social agencies in the community. In a system of several homes such as Community Homes, this information can be obtained from the director who informs the housemanagers about the available resources and agencies in the community. If the housemanagers are replacing housemanagers in an on-going rather than a new home, sometimes the residents of the community home can be quite helpful in contributing some of the information to the new housemanagers. When housemanagers find themselves in a newly developed home with no director or system of several existing homes, they will have to seek out community agencies and develop new liaisons for these sources (see Chapter 4).

The training of housemanagers to implement behavioral programs is multidimensional and occurs in different ways. Most of the training is informal and resembles an on-the-job training situation rather than a formal instructional setting. The training of housemanagers is viewed as a continuous process along with the continuous rehabilitation of the community home residents.

Some of our housemanagers have been trained in special education and/or have had experience working with retarded people. Although this previous training or experience may facilitate training, it is not necessary in order to teach people to become effective housemanagers. Although our sample of housemanagers is small, we have not found differences in effectiveness between those housemanagers who had previous experience working with the retarded and those who have not had this experience. What appears to be more important is the quality of the housemanager rather than their previous training or experience.

One component of the training program involves the use of behavior modification workshops. Approximately twice a year, this author, as the consulting psychologist for the program, meets with all of the housemanagers to review principles of behavior modification. After these principles are reviewed, specific behavioral problems are introduced and various behavioral approaches for dealing with the problems are discussed. Such discussions give the housemanagers opportunities to see how other housemanagers deal with behavioral problems, to view how one problem can be approached in different ways, to enjoy the considerable degree of ingenuity and creativity that is involved in using behavior modification, and to learn how other housemanagers are dealing with behaviors that are similar to those expressed by their own residents. One of the consequences of these discussions is that housemanagers develop additional confidence in themselves and the approach and are apt to be more independent and comfortable in employing behavior modification procedures when problems arise.

Role-playing is also used at these workshops and is viewed as a helpful and powerful technique to drive home principles of behavior modification. In these role-playing situations, one housemanager role plays a particular behavior of a resident that is to be changed and another housemanager plays him or herself. Traditional as well as possible new ways of approaching a particular situation are role played and discussed by the housemanagers. One of the many learning opportunities afforded by roleplaying is that it clearly demonstrates how housemanagers may be encouraging or reinforcing a particular behavior that they are trying to eliminate in a resident.

Training of housemanagers also occurs within the weekly house meeting with the residents. Twice a month, the house meeting is directed by this author. By observing and possibly identifying with the author, the housemanagers learn skills in directing a group meeting and in understanding group and individual behaviors. On alternate weeks, the housemanagers direct the group meeting themselves, which thus gives them opportunities and practice in dealing with group, individual, and house matters.

Another opportunity for training occurs when housemanagers and assistants meet with this author to review the progress of residents. These meetings take place twice a month. The meeting affords opportunities to discuss behavioral goals and implementation of these goals. Subjects and problems that could not be discussed at the house meeting are also discussed.

Finally and perhaps most useful to the housemanagers is the availability of both the director and psychological consultant to deal with emergencies, problems, and difficult situations when they arise. Usually, these matters can be solved over the phone with some discussion. Other times, the director and/or consultant are at any house within five minutes to assist the housemanager in a difficult situation. This availability brings support to the housemanagers, who, in time, develop sufficient confidence to deal with these problems themselves. We now assume, with some supportive evidence, that housemanagers, when working in a system that has several community homes, begin to rely on other housemanagers for support and advice when difficult situations arise.

Duties and Responsibilities

The housemanagers are responsible for the general health, education, and welfare of the residents in the home. In a way, these responsibilities are no different from the obligations that all responsible parents have towards their dependents. And like parents, the housemanagers must provide opportunities that will enable the residents to take care of themselves eventually. Housemanagers must also foster the development of a resident's educational, vocational, and recreational opportunities.

When a community home first begins, the housemanagers spend an unusual amount of time devoted to the general health of the residents. Formerly institutionalized people appear to receive minimal health care and certainly not the quality of care received by most middle-class people in the United States. Therefore, upon the resident's arrival in the community home, appointments must be made to see a doctor for a general examination, a dentist, opthamologist, or other specialists such as those who fit people for hearing aids, prosthetic devices, and so forth. An appointment with a psychiatrist is necessary to determine whether the medication the resident received at the institution is still necessary or needs to be changed. In general, we have assumed that in many cases—although there are exceptions—the health care received in institutions is less than adequate. Housemanagers rely less on past medical records received from the institutions and seem to have more confidence in the professionals who work in the community.

Housemanagers also serve as an important resource for the resident's varied interests and needs. Managers should be able to offer information about applying for a driver's license or for a job in the community, signing up for adult education courses, or going about earning a high school diploma. In general, housemanagers serve as advocates for the residents in providing them with needed information and advice that is unavailable to them or that they cannot obtain by themselves (see Chapter 4).

In addition to being responsible for the general welfare of the residents, housemanagers are also responsible for the general physical maintenance of the house. The responsibilities associated with the maintenance of the house are no different from those of any homeowner, except that housemanagers do not have to be concerned with mortgage payments or taxes. Housemanagers are responsible for the upkeep and attractiveness of the exterior and interior of the house and must ensure that the house is a comfortable, enjoyable place to live.

The day-to-day activities of running a home are also the responsibility of the housemanagers. Some of these responsibilities include purchasing food and supplies, keeping the house safe and clean, repairing appliances, making household repairs, and so forth. Housemanagers not only assume responsibility for eight to ten residents but also inherit the responsibility of running an entire and unusually large house.

Rehabilitative and behavioral programs for each resident are developed by the housemanager in conjunction with the psychological consultant and the director of the program. The housemanagers are responsible for implementing the programs, reviewing them, and communicating the degree of success and progress of these programs. Housemanagers are asked to continuously change certain behavioral goals once these goals have been reached by a resident.

A communication commitment is also required of the housemanagers. This commitment involves keeping various personnel and community agencies informed about important changes or problems in the house or with the residents. The personnel and agencies involved include the program director, the consulting psychologist, the institution referring the resident, vocational rehabilitation personnel, and the various state and federal agencies serving a particular resident.

There are many administrative responsibilities associated with the housemanager position. Monthly rent from each resident must be collected and recorded, medical and behavioral records must be maintained and updated, and various federal and state applications and documents must be handled by the housemanager when these forms cannot be completed by the resident.

Housemanagers are given the responsibility of hiring and supervising their assistant housemanagers. Since they must live in the same house and work closely with one another, selecting an assistant seems most reasonably done by the housemanager.

The assistant housemanager, like the housemanager, lives in the house with the residents. The assistant's primary role is to function as a housemanager when the latter is away. The assistant knows the residents and the routines in the house as well as the housemanager and therefore is quite capable of taking care of the house in the housemanager's absence.

The assistants and housemanagers usually alternate their scheduled time-off or time away from the house. This alternation might involve the assistants taking two days off every other weekend, with the housemanagers taking the alternate weekends off. Evenings off during the week are alternated in a similar way. Relieving the housemanagers and giving them free time *away* from the home is viewed as extremely important both for the housemanager and the functioning of the home. Replacing housemanagers with assistant housemanagers who know and live with the residents is more meaningful than bringing in strangers or a second "institutional shift" of personnel to run the house while the housemanagers are away. Thus, there is always some coverage in the home by a responsible person who knows both the residents and the functioning of the home.

Some demographic information describing the assistant housemanagers in our program is presented in Table 6–2. Most of the assistants are in their twenties and come from a variety of socioeconomic and religious backgrounds. They are usually college graduates who have majored in the social sciences. With one exception, the assistant housemanagers are unmarried. Most of the assistants have not had previous experience working with retarded people, which is in contrast to the fact that half of our housemanagers have had such prior experiences. Assistants usually keep their jobs for 18 months or more and learn about the position in the same informal ways as do the housemanagers.

The importance of the salary and benefits offered to housemanagers should be underscored. When the budget for a community home is tight, skimping on the furniture is preferred to skimping on the housemanager's salary. As every prudent employer knows, you only get what you pay for. By offering a good salary, a greater number of highly qualified people are likely to apply for the position, and a good salary would influence a housemanager's decision to keep the job after a given period of time.

In January 1974, we hired three housemanager couples at an annual salary of $11,000 plus benefits. The benefits include room and board, social security, unemployment compensation, workman's compensation, and basic and major medical health insurance. This compensation seemed to attract a good number of candidates for the position.

Compensation for assistant housemanagers includes a salary of $3,100 and benefits such as room and board, social security, workman's compensation, and basic and major medical health insurance. Some homes, like the children's houses, require more staff—additional assistants who live in and

Table 6-2
Demographic Information on Live-In Assistants [a]

Assistant	Sex	Age	Father's or Mother's Highest Income (M)	Religion	Education	Major	Marital Status	Past Experience Working with Retarded People	Previous Work Experience	Length of Time Served as Assistant	Way in Which Learned about Assistant Position
1	M	22	12	Unitarian	BA	Psychology	S	No	Library Assistant	13 Mos.	Previous Asst.
2	M	25	50	Methodist	BA	Anthropology	S	No	Busboy	Presently Employed	Previous Asst.
3	M	24	19	R. Catholic	BA	Sociology	S	No	Rehab. Superv.	Presently Employed	Friend
4	M	24			1½	L.A.	S	No	Carpenter	Presently Employed	Newspaper
5	M	23	65	R. Catholic	BA	Sociology	S	No	O.R. Service Clerk	10 Mos.	Friends
6	M	30	13	Quaker	BS	Psychology	S	No	Teacher	Presently Employed	Rehab Workshop
7	M	24			BA	Psychology	S	No	Hosp. Attend.	7 Mos.	Friends
8	F	25	25	Jewish	MEd.	El. Ed.	S	Yes	Teacher	Presently Employed	Friends
9	M	23	14	Quaker	2 yrs.	Hum.Potent.	M	No	Various Odd Jobs	Presently Employed	Religious Meeting
10	F	23	8	R. Catholic	1 yr.	Mental Hlth.	S	No	Hospital Aid	10 Days	Friends
11	M	31	30	Jewish	1 yr.		S	No	Merchant Marine	Presently Employed	Friends, also Housemanagers

[a] At the time hired.

also assistants who work just during the day and weekends. The annual salary for the day assistants is $6,000.

At the time of being hired, housemanagers are told that they are expected to take the position for a minimum of one year. No formally written contracts are made and the housemanagers are given the assurance of keeping the position during that year providing nothing drastic occurs such as a display of bizarre or reckless judgment that seriously disrupts the home situation and the welfare of the residents. Should such a situation arise, it is agreed that housemanagers would be asked to resign.

Following an eight-month period of employment, housemanagers are given a written evaluation of their performance as housemanagers from the director. The evaluation describes the housemanager's strengths and weaknesses in a positive spirit so that the housemanagers can use the evaluation as a learning experience. Similar evaluations of assistant housemanagers are made by the housemanagers. These are given to the assistants in order to let them know how well they are doing and, again, to provide potential learning experiences. Opportunity is provided for both the housemanagers and the assistants to discuss their written evaluations with their respective evaluators to clarify questions or issues of concern to either party.

References

Gilberstadt, H. and Duker, J. 1965. *A Handbook for Clinical and Actuarial MMPI Interpretation*. Philadelphia: W. B. Saunders.

Hathaway, S. R. and McKinley, J. C. 1943. *The Minnesota Multiphasic Personality Inventory*. New York: The Psychological Corporation.

Marks, P. A. and Sines, J. O. 1969. "Methodological Problems of Cookbook Construction," in J. N. Butcher, ed., *MMPI: Research Developments and Clinical Applications*. New York: McGraw-Hill. Pp. 71–96.

Nirje, B. 1969. "The Normalization Principle," in R. Kugel and W. Wolfensberger, eds., *Changing Patterns in Residential Services for the Mentally Retarded*. Washington, D.C.: President's Committee on Mental Retardation.

7

Behavioral Programs
Joel S. Bergman

Behavioral Goals and Orientation

Community homes are viewed as settings for fostering the development of new skills and interests that will be valuable to the residents and that will enhance their educational, vocational, and recreational opportunities. The homes are seen as having rehabilitative function in focusing on the development of each resident's potential and in developing skills that will lead to a more independent, productive, meaningful, and rich life.

The overall orientation of the program is to provide the resident with learning opportunities that will lead to the maximally developed skills necessary to live independently in the community. These skills will, of course, vary with each particular resident. Some of the skills considered important for further development are the following: independent functioning; social and sexual functioning; vocational development; physical development; domestic skills; language development; economic activities; and the development of self-direction and responsibility.

The program is also oriented towards having the resident maximally involved with other residents in the home as well as becoming actively involved with and integrated in the community. The homes are oriented towards providing an atmosphere that is no different from any other home —that is, a familiar, comfortable place where one lives, separate from where one works, with a given number of people, and also a learning setting in which less skillful, more dependent individuals are taught to be more skillful and independent. It is also expected, that like any other home, community homes will have their share of fighting, jealousies, favoring, competition, and other phenomena that makes home life so colorful, emotionally charged, and dynamic.

Description of the Residents

Before describing some of the behavioral approaches found to be successful in the program, it is important to describe the residents since behavioral approaches vary with the level of functioning of a particular resident. Individual levels of functioning in this book are described in the form of scores on various behavioral dimensions of the *Adaptive Behavior Scale* (*ABS*) (1974). The *ABS* is used because it describes overt behaviors in quantified form and compares these behaviors to a standardized group of institutionalized retarded people. Scores from I.Q. tests are not reported since their interpretation deals more with covert processes rather than overt behavior. In addition, the usefulness of I.Q. scores is presently restricted to predicting academic success, which is not very useful to the residents nor to the program.

Tables 7–1 through 7–6 present some descriptive information about the residents in the adult and children community homes. Scores on the *Adaptive Behavior Scale* are given in deciles to permit a comparison between a community home resident and a standardized group of institutionalized retarded individuals along different behavioral dimensions.

The majority of the adult residents (except where noted) in our program were referred from a large (over 1,000 census) state school for the retarded. Many have spent over two-thirds of their life in this institution. The few individuals who were not referred from the state school either came directly from the community, were referred from a state hospital for "epileptics," or came from a state mental hospital.

The Crescent Street house was the first community home established in our program and has been in existence about two and one-half years. Since this home was also one of the first established in a particular cachement area in Massachusetts, the first group of residents placed in the home from the state school showed considerable degrees of autonomy and developed skills. The high level of functioning in this first group is partially demonstrated by the *ABS* scores of the residents *presently* living at Crescent Street that are illustrated in Table 7–1. Residents in the original group placed into Crescent Street who are not described in Table 7–1 either went back to the state school or are presently living independently in the community. Their scores are in Table 7–7.

From the high *ABS* scores and the success with which people from Crescent Street have been placed into independent living situations, it appears that the first group of residents referred from the state school were the most independent and highly functioning residents at the state school. As state schools continue to place their residents into community homes, there will probably be a relative decline in the degree of autonomy and level of functioning of these residents compared to the original group placed into Crescent Street.

As is probably true with most success stories, the moment word got around the community that there was an effective community home for retarded individuals established in town, referrals started pouring in from other agencies who were dealing with populations of clients other than the retarded. Requests to place clients into Crescent Street came from the

Table 7-1

Adaptive Behavior Scale Scores (percentile)
Crescent Street House (males)

Resident	Age	Years of Institutionalization	Independent Functioning	Physical Development	Economic Activity	Language Development	Numbers & Time	Domestic Activity	Vocational Activity	Self-Direction	Responsibility	Socialization
			Behavioral Scales									
A [b]	45	20	52	22	98	82	98	98	75	78	45	22
B	23	17	82	98	99	65	85	99	98	98	99	95
C	49	34	75	36	99	99	98	99	98	98	98	99
D	21	15	85	98	99	75	85	98	58	98	99	92
E	42	27	90	99	99	92	98	85	98	98	86	90
F	30	21	94	99	99	88	98	99	55	98	85	90
G [a]	45		90	99	99	90	98	99	98	98	85	95
H	55	43	80	98	99	32	85	99	98	98	98	98
I [b]	33	8	94	57	99	98	70	85	98	98	72	90

[a] Never Institutionalized.
[b] State Mental Hospital.

state mental hospital, the jail, probation officials, and from some families in the community who were experiencing a family crisis situation "caused" by some individual in that particular family.

Since the Crescent Street house at that time was established with no direct state funds and with no direct mandate to provide services solely to retarded individuals, the house often accepted people referred from these agencies when there was an opening. Although the behavioral program initially established at Crescent Street was geared and directed towards retarded individuals from the state school, it was assumed that other populations of people being referred from other agencies would also benefit from such a behavioral program. This assumption turned out to be naive and basically incorrect.

Within the two and one-half years that the Crescent Street house has been in existence, there have been approximately twenty unsuccessful placements into the community home from the state mental hospital. Most state hospital patients returned to the state hospital within a period of two or three days, although we have had about five patients for about four months, and two individuals, presently living at Crescent Street, for 12 and 36 months, respectively.

In retrospect, the atmosphere established at Crescent Street was probably too open-ended, permissive, and democratic for state hospital patients when compared to the favorable responses this atmosphere elicits with state school residents. The two successful placements from the state hospital can be attributed to the way in which these two individuals behave when they become upset. When upset, these individuals become depressed, withdrawn, and passive, which is tolerated by the other residents in the home and which is also quickly ameliorated by a recontinuation or change in medication. The unsuccessful placements from the state hospital can also be attributed to these individuals' behavior when upset. When these patients regress or begin displaying acute behaviors such as agitation, aggressiveness, verbalizations of their hallucinations and delusions, these behaviors produce a great deal of fear and tension in the other residents in the house, which usually is not tolerated for long by the residents, the housemanagers, or the state hospital patients themselves. Thus, considering the specific type of atmosphere and programs developed at Crescent Street, only certain types of state hospital patients can be placed successfully in such a program at the present time.

Our experience with ex-offenders is limited to two individuals and very little can be concluded on why the program at Crescent Street was not effective with these individuals. In both cases, these individuals ran away from the house after committing an offense or after their probationary period was up. The programs cited in *Halfway Houses* (Keller and Alper 1970) are probably more applicable to these individuals than the present programs and approaches established at Crescent Street.

Approximately ten months ago, in January 1974, three new community homes for adults were established for individuals formerly living in a state school for the retarded. These homes were funded by the state solely for retarded individuals from the state school. All three homes were located in one cachement area of the state and accepted people from the state school who lived in this cachement area prior to institutionalization.

One of these new homes was established on Elm Street and consists of eight male residents. Table 7–2 provides some descriptive information about these residents along with scores from the *Adaptive Behavior Scale*. It is noteworthy to point out the differences in *ABS* scores between Elm Street residents and residents at Crescent Street, the latter having left the institution about two years prior to the Elm Street residents. These differences are even more evident when one looks at Table 7–5, which provides mean *ABS* scores for the four different adult homes. The differences in scores between these two homes, suggest the obvious—that is, as more people leave the state school, the level of functioning of these residents is lower than previously released residents. The *ABS* scores in Table 7–2 also suggest that there is considerable variability between and within individuals with respect to level of functioning and the acquisition of different skills. This variability between individuals is not viewed as creating problems, since there are individual programs for each resident. In addition, having a group of people whose skills vary considerably approaches a more family-like situation that would include members of a family who differ in age, skills, and different levels of autonomy.

The Center Street house was established in January 1974 and was one of the first homes for women in a particular cachement area. Table 7–3 provides some information about these individuals and also includes the *ABS* scores. All the women in this home (except where noted) also came from the state school. The mean *ABS* scores for this home are slightly higher than scores from the Elm Street or Bridge Street homes, because Center Street was the first community home for women in the cachement area and probably drew more independent women with more developed skills from the state school. (See Table 7–5 for comparisons of mean scores.)

Bridge Street is the last of the recently established homes, and some descriptive data and the *ABS* scores are given in Table 7–4. Bridge Street is the first of the four adult community homes permitted to accept people who formerly lived in a state hospital for epileptics. Note how drastically different the *ABS* scores in Table 7–4 are for the three individuals from this hospital compared with the residents who formerly lived at the state school for the retarded.

Some interesting implications result from looking at the *ABS* scores of the residents living in the Elm Street (Table 7–2) and Bridge Street (Table 7–4) homes. On two important behavioral dimensions called "In-

Table 7-2
Adaptive Behavior Scale Scores (percentile)
Elm Street House (males)

Resident	Age	Years of Institutionalization	Behavioral Scales									
			Independent Functioning	Physical Development	Economic Activity	Language Development	Numbers & Time	Domestic Activity	Vocational Activity	Self-Direction	Responsibility	Socialization
A	25	15	49	70	90	60	80	88	38	68	45	80
B	50	22	92	80	99	98	85	98	98	99	98	80
C	28	22	49	22	85	75	65	82	58	68	45	72
D	48	34	75	38	75	41	29	95	75	68	98	80
E	26	10	49	98	82	58	53	79	42	55	99	65
F	38	24	80	98	99	98	98	92	75	78	98	55
G	36	32	52	48	83	62	55	80	75	05	98	48
H	40	32	48	18	68	30	38	80	38	18	85	90

Table 7-3

Adaptive Behavior Scale Scores (percentile)
Center Street House (females)

Resident	Age	Years of Institutionalization	Behavioral Scales									
			Independent Functioning	Physical Development	Economic Activity	Language Development	Numbers & Time	Domestic Activity	Vocational Activity	Self-Direction	Responsibility	Socialization
A	23	17	75	99	92	80	85	98	98	68	99	72
B	30	21	93	98	99	92	98	99	75	53	98	85
C	36	13	42	98	55	72	70	85	55	35	72	48
D	41	27	65	98	88	68	60	99	98	98	98	98
E [a]	19		39	98	82	42	55	88	48	78	70	95
F	30	21	75	98	88	55	60	99	35	35	85	65
G	46	21	80	37	98	88	70	99	38	66	85	95
H	36	16	65	98	84	69	60	99	98	55	98	95

[a] Never institutionalized.

Table 7–4

Adaptive Behavior Scale Scores (percentile)
Bridge Street House (males)

Resident	Age	Years of Institutionalization	Behavioral Scales									
			Independent Functioning	Physical Development	Economic Activity	Language Development	Numbers & Time	Domestic Activity	Vocational Activity	Self-Direction	Responsibility	Socialization
A	48	34	29	10	48	22	20	60	32	23	35	40
B	51	36	38	80	78	30	22	85	53	38	86	55
C [a]	31	10	99	48	99	92	98	95	98	98	98	55
D [a]	58	18	99	80	99	99	85	98	98	98	99	89
E [a]	36	23	95	56	99	92	98	95	55	78	86	80
F	47	33	52	58	59	47	45	95	75	66	85	65
G	42	28	45	18	58	26	20	70	38	10	35	48
H	46	29	48	58	75	72	55	75	75	66	72	98

[a] From state hospital for epileptics.

dependent Functioning" and "Language Development," half the residents in both homes have *ABS* scores on these two dimensions that are below the 50 percentile level. Scoring below the 50 percentile level suggests that 50 percent of the people *presently institutionalized* at state schools would obtain higher scores on "Independent Functioning" and "Language Development." Since our residents with scores below 50 percent are doing quite well living in community homes, one implication from observing these scores is that perhaps 50 percent of the people presently living at state schools would do just as well, if not better, living in community homes.

Putting this argument in a different way, half the residents who are presently living in the Elm and Bridge Street homes would probably be labeled "severely retarded" in certain circles. There are probably many people presently living in institutions who also would be considered "severely retarded" and who are not being recommended for community placement because they are "severely retarded." We are saying that we have "severely retarded" people living in community homes and they are doing well. This seems to be a convincing argument that the vast majority of people living in institutions have no reason to be there and that they could be living successfully in the community.

The community home for children was established in January 1972 and was the first community home for children in Massachusetts. Table 7–6 provides some information about these children and also presents the *ABS* scores for these individuals. The variation in levels of functioning is considerable within this group, particularly with three of these children (A, F, and G) who show many less-developed skills than the remaining children. Because of these differences in level of development and because these three individuals were not getting as much time and programming from the housemanagers in the first children's home, another community home for children was established in August 1974 for these three children and similar children whose needs and level of development require more time, staffing, and programming. Thus, two homes have been established to deal with children who are functioning at different levels of development, which require settings that vary considerably in staffing and programming patterns. The adult community home programs are probably more suited to deal effectively with people who vary in level of functioning than are the children's homes.

The residents in our program were discharged from the institutions in groups of three to five individuals, and each house was completely occupied within a period of two weeks. Placing a group of people into a community home has several advantages over individual placements. First, the transition to a new way of life is probably easier because the residents retain their familiarity with each other, and the transition seems easier for them when made with familiar people. Teaching people new routines and pro-

Table 7-5

Mean Adaptive Behavior Scale Scores (percentile) Adult Homes

Name of House	Age	Years of Institutionalization	Behavioral Scales									
			Independent Functioning	Physical Development	Economic Activity	Language Development	Time & Numbers	Domestic Activity	Vocational Activity	Self-Direction	Responsibility	Socialization
Elm	36	25	60	48	88	68	65	88	55	52	85	72
Bridge	45	26	58	38	83	66	55	85	55	52	72	72
Crescent	38	22	82	58	99	80	98	95	75	98	85	90
Center	33	20	62	99	88	72	65	95	75	55	85	85

Table 7-6

Adaptive Behavior Scale Scores (percentile)
Children's Home

Resident	Sex	Age	Years of Institutionalization	Independent Functioning	Physical Development	Economic Activity	Language Development	Time & Numbers	Domestic Activity	Vocational Activity	Self-Direction	Responsibility	Socialization
										Behavioral Scales			
A	M	19		05	12	24	11	15	15	22	20	22	03
B	M	12		75	65	85	85	99	92	65	72	95	82
C	M	16		55	98	42	47	70	95	97	69	92	59
D	F	13		52	65	49	65	78	85	70	69	80	98
E	F	16		22	32	37	10	62	48	35	45	46	69
F	M	10		0	15	49	22	28	25	42	01	39	09
G	M	11		03	15	49	22	28	25	64	05	39	39
H	M	12		78	52	99	92	99	99	46	59	65	89

cedures is also easier when an entire group has to learn these new ways. Our experience suggests, perhaps for reasons other than the above, that individuals who are placed one at a time into a home have more difficulty adjusting to a community home life than people who are placed as a group into a community home.

The criteria for judging when a state school resident is ready for a community home are, from this author's point of view, vague and non-specific. When the state school was informed that community homes were taking individuals, residents were probably selected on the basis of an individual being motivated to live in the community and "ready" for placement. Judging from the variation in age, chronicity, and behavior of the residents in each home (see Tables 7–1 through 7–4), being "ready" for placement probably constituted different things to different staff members at the state school. Nevertheless, the variety of ages and levels of development of members in a community home has not been a problem and constitutes a refreshing contrast to the age-segregated stratification that occurs in society.

Criteria for accepting and maintaining a resident in a community home once referred by the state school are equally non-specific. The program for the four adult homes has been quite liberal about accepting and keeping incoming residents who display a variety of behavioral problems. Within the two and one-half years since the first community home was developed, no resident has ever been asked to leave the home because of behavioral problems. Two rules, however, exist that can lead to expulsion from the home. One has to do with violent behavior directed towards people or property. The other has to do with stealing. A resident is first given a warning when either behavior occurs, and then is asked to leave the community home when the behavior is repeated. The use of these two rules has never led to asking any resident to leave the home. When violence or stealing is observed, the individual is given the warning, and a behavioral program is immediately devised and implemented (see section on programs) to eliminate the violence or stealing.

Individual Behavioral Programs

When residents first arrive at the community home, they are informed about the house rules and the responsibilities involved in living in a community home. The house rules are few and include the above mentioned rules on stealing and violence. In addition, in order to remain in the home, residents must be employed in some vocational setting, whether it takes the form of a sheltered workshop or competitive employment.

Responsibilities include one's own personal hygiene, the upkeep of one's room, and doing one of the household chores. Each member has one household job that is rotated every two weeks. The rotation is performed to maintain fairness since some household chores are more difficult and time-consuming than others. In addition, this rotation allows members to learn about the necessary jobs in a home in order to keep the home safe, clean, and comfortable.

Residents are also responsible for preparing their bag lunches for work and for the preparation and serving of one evening meal each week. Residents who are inexperienced with the preparation of food are paired with a more experienced resident or with a housemanager until they develop sufficient skills to prepare meals by themselves. Meals are expected to be served on time, varied from one week to another, and interesting. In one of the more advanced houses, residents write a menu for the following week and indicate to the housemanagers the necessary ingredients for their planned meals. The purchases are then made by the housemanagers.

A behavioral chart is developed and maintained for each resident (see Appendix B). The chart consists of five behavioral goals that the resident is to work towards or achieve. The chart describes the specific behaviors to be developed or eliminated, means of developing these behaviors, and a weekly evaluation of whether the resident is making progress towards these goals. The goals are determined during periodic conferences between the resident and the housemanagers and the psychological consultant. After certain goals have been attained, the chart is revised to include new goals the resident wishes to achieve.

The behavioral chart serves many purposes. First, it gives the housemanager and the resident a specific, concrete set of goals to work towards. The weekly review of progress reminds the housemanager of the goals for each resident, so the housemanager is more likely to reinforce these behaviors when they are observed in everyday encounters with the resident. The chart also provides a permanent record of a resident's progress and gives the community home staff some idea as to which behavioral approaches are effective, or ineffective, with each individual resident.

Implementation of Behavioral Goals

Most of the behavioral goals placed on the behavior chart are implemented with the use of behavior modification principles (Thompson and Gabrowski 1972). Stated in an oversimplified manner, behavior that is ignored should, in time, occur less frequently, and behavior that is rewarded should occur more frequently. One of the problems with a behavior modification approach in a natural setting (Reppucci and Saunders 1974) is that at times it is virtually impossible to ignore a behavior you wish to extinguish, and conversely, it is sometimes very difficult to find rewards that a resident will work to obtain. The following sequence is the approach we have successfully employed in using principles of behavior modification to implement goals on resident's behavioral charts.

In general, we find that positive reinforcement works more effectively than negative reinforcement, and therefore most of our attempts to implement new goals are based on the use of positive reinforcement. The first step in the sequence of attempts to change behavior is simply to ask or direct the resident to do the new behavior. In many cases, directing the resident to the new behavior and reinforcing that behavior when it occurs with social reinforcement (smiling, compliments, physical affection) is sufficient for many behaviors to be developed and maintained.

When social reinforcement does not seem to be effective, we begin to think about other sources of positive reinforcement. Sometimes one can come across an effective reward by talking to the resident and discussing the kinds of things the resident likes to do. Sources of reinforcement can also be found by observing what the resident does with a high frequency (Premack 1959), which is assuming that a person doing something quite often finds that activity rewarding. One might attempt to reinforce the new behavior (target behavior) by providing the opportunity for the resident to engage in a high-frequency-occurring behavior *following* the occurrence of the target behavior.

In many cases, basic types of reinforcers such as money or food do not seem applicable. When residents are receiving SSI funds "for being handicapped," they are in ways, being reinforced for being "handicapped" or "retarded" or "dependent." Since the community home program cannot provide greater sums of money for acting appropriately than the residents' receive from the Social Security Administration for being inappropriate, rewards other than money have to be considered. Food is also not as appropriate a reward as some textbooks suggest, since many of the residents discharged from state schools are overweight, and many are placed on diets to lose weight once they are placed in a community home.

Finding rewards that are unique to the resident takes time, experimentation, and considerable creativity, but is nevertheless worth the time and energy expended since shaping behaviors with positive reinforcement is less complicated and seems more effective than using negative reinforcement. Sometimes the unique rewards take the form of spending extra time with a housemanager; being taken out to lunch or dinner by the housemanager, an assistant, the psychological consultant or director of the program; going out for a beer with a staff member; spending a day or weekend traveling with a staff member. Once these rewards are determined, they can be placed on some hierarchy of value and contracted for with the resident.

Behavioral contracts are useful when there are several behavioral goals simultaneously planned for a particular resident. In order for the contract to be effective several conditions must be met. First the goals should be clearly and explicitly stated in written form, and assurances should be made that the resident can understand these goals. It is also important that the resident can simultaneously work on these goals. Third, the behaviors to be sought must be observable, and when a resident displays a new behavior, a point (if a point contract is used) should be given immediately following the observation of that new behavior.

The contract must also explicitly state the reward or pay-off involved after a resident achieves a given, agreed upon number of points. It is best to start off with a small time period (say, 1 or 2 days) and a lowered number of points necessary to receive the pay-off. Once the contract appears to be working, the time period and number of points necessary to receive the reward can be extended.

Contracts are convenient ways of dealing with several behavioral goals at the same time. Distributing points rather than concrete tangible rewards is also more convenient. The contract also more closely approximates the types of agreements adults enter into in society and provide learning experiences towards the delay of immediate gratification.

Contracts should explicitly state the terms under which they are to be terminated. When many different goals are being considered for an individual resident, after certain goals are reached and the behaviors appear stable, new goals should replace the old goals in the form of a renegotiated contract. Also, renegotiation is sometimes necessary to change the rewards involved in the contract, since some adaptation to the contract and the rewards is inevitable.

The elimination of undesirable or inappropriate behaviors can occur in different ways, and some approaches seem to work more effectively with some residents than with other residents. This author views a great deal of the inappropriate behavior found in formerly institutionalized populations as maladaptive means of getting attention. Consequently, maladaptive ways of getting attention can be completely ignored (extinction), and the resident is taught to obtain attention with appropriate behaviors.

Bizarre or inappropriate language, sounds, or gestures can best be eliminated quite efficiently by totally ignoring these behaviors. We have gone so far as to instruct other residents in the homes to ignore some of these inappropriate behaviors and have achieved considerable success with the cooperation from the residents. When considering the extinction of a behavior, it is always helpful to consider the appropriate alternatives to replace the inappropriate behavior and to encourage and reward these appropriate alternatives while concurrently ignoring the inappropriate behavior. It is also helpful to find appropriate alternative behaviors that are incompatible with the behavior being extinguished.

Certain inappropriate behaviors cannot be eliminated by extinction procedures for a host of different reasons. Sometimes the behavior is so provocative or obnoxious that it is almost impossible not to respond to it, and therefore the behavior is reinforced with the attention it provokes.

One resident had a habit of slamming his bedroom door very loudly and late in the evening when the sound was quite disruptive to most people. After many unsuccessful attempts through reason to get him to be more considerate of others, we warned him that if he slammed the door in a disruptive way again, we would remove the door from his room for a period of two weeks. Soon after he slammed his door, whereupon we removed the door. Two weeks after removing the door from the hinges, the door was replaced with no re-currences of door slamming.

Behaviors that provoke irritation or anger in other residents are very hard to eliminate by ignoring the provocative behavior. Residents will co-operate with the housemanagers' request to ignore a particular behavior of another resident to a point, beyond which leads to the residents' responding to the inappropriate behavior in some way.

Another resident had the habit of "accidentally" bumping into other residents while walking or at the dinner table. He also had the habit of making a tre-mendous racket in the kitchen at 6 A.M. while he was "preparing" breakfast. After repeated requests to be more considerate of others, which went un-heeded, we decided to set up a contract that we called the "bumping contract." The contract stated that whenever anyone was "accidentally" bumped by this fellow, the latter would be charged 25¢ per bump. Twenty-five cents would be the penalty for each bumping offense, and the resident could have all the collected fines returned to him if he could spend two entire weeks without committing any bumping infraction. Needless to say, we never collected one quarter. This contract was so effective that we tried to eliminate the noise made at 6 A.M. by changing the contract to an "annoyance contract" where a quarter fine would be collected for a behavior that others felt was annoying such as bumping or making a racket at 6 A.M. The annoyance contract worked, and people in the house not only found themselves bumped less frequently, but were able to wake up in the morning to their alarm clocks rather than to the "sounds of breakfast being prepared."

Behaviors that are self-mutilating also cannot be eliminated by ignoring the behavior for obvious humanitarian reasons. When self-mutilating be-haviors are observed, a program is immediately or quickly devised for eliminating the behavior.

When one of our female residents became upset, she often would bite her arm. This self-mutilating habit was well-developed and went on for years while she was in a state school. Talking to her about this habit was fruitless; since she was quite embarrassed about this behavior, in talking about it, she made believe it didn't occur. Placing skin lotion on the arm (hoping it would have a bad taste) worked for a while, but the resident would revert to arm-biting when she experienced tension. We assumed that the arm-biting was associated with tension, or the reduction of tension, so we concentrated on trying to develop more appropriate ways of reducing the tension other than arm-biting. Trying to teach her to relax the moment she felt the urge to bite was suggested (Webster and Azrin 1973). We told her to go up and relax in her bed whenever she felt the urge to bite her arm. This suggestion was very hard for her to understand and difficult for the housemanager to implement. Finally, we started thinking of behaviors that could replace the arm-biting and that were also incompatible with arm-biting. The resident loved cookies and donuts. Our thought was that she preferred biting cookies to biting her arm and that she could not eat cookies and bite her arm at the same time. So, we told her that whenever she felt the urge to bite her arm, she should get a cookie and take a bite instead. In a way, one could argue that the cookie reinforced the urge to bite the arm. On the other hand one could argue that the cookie reinforced control of not biting the arm and seeking a cookie instead. In addition, we told her that she could earn a cookie at the end of the day if she did not bite her arm for the entire day. So far this program to stop arm-biting behavior seems to be working since its inception six weeks ago. Finally, the resident appears to be quite proud of the control she has developed over her arm-biting behavior, which is believed to have caused embarrassment to the resident.

Besides using positive reinforcement and extinction as means of changing behavior, we have also found that negative reinforcement procedures are effective with certain individuals. Usually the negative reinforcement approaches are considered after all other attempts to change behavior have failed, and it appears from our limited experience that some residents respond more favorably to negative reinforcement than to positive reinforcement approaches.

A negative reinforcement contract was used quite successfully in helping an obese resident lose weight when the individual requested assistance in losing weight.

One of our residents who was mildly retarded and had a history of prolonged hospitalizations for psychotic behavior indicated that he was interested in losing weight. Not only was he 150 pounds overweight, but it was thought that the extra pounds contributed to his passive, inactive lifestyle and to his negative self-concept. We obviously could not use food as reinforcement, but we knew that money was very important to this individual, and therefore devised a weight-reducing contract that included money. The contract consisted of an agreement, between the resident and the housemanager, that 2 pounds would be lost each week and if the resident gained, stayed even, or lost only one pound, he would give the housemanagers the sum of five dollars. The five dollars would be placed in a "weight contract trust fund" in a bank, and the resident could collect all the deposited funds when he reached 180 pounds, which was approximately the appropriate weight for his height and frame. Once the contract began, he lost weight for the first three or four weeks. In the fifth week, he did not lose the two pounds, and he continued to have to pay five dollars to the housemanagers for the next few weeks. Not being upset when he had to pay the housemanagers bothered us. We knew money was important to this individual; yet the resident was not losing weight and gladly paying the money. At first we thought the contract was not going to work, but one day we received a call from the resident's sister-in-law. The sister-in-law complained about the resident's accusations that we were taking his money, and with further inquiry, we learned that the sister-in-law and her husband were giving the resident five dollars "under the table" whenever he visited them, which had turned into a weekly routine. After explaining our contract to the resident's family, and receiving their cooperation in not giving him any money for any reason, the contract started working as expected. The resident started getting quite angry over paying the five dollars, and within a period of six months, he lost over 60 pounds.

One of the behavioral programs involving negative reinforcement was used to help an individual resident develop more effective means of keeping himself, his clothes, and his room clean. The program was so effective and apparently engaging to the other residents in the house that we applied this technique to any resident who would not keep himself, his clothes, or his room clean after reminders and positive reinforcement approachs failed. We euphemistically called this behavioral program "the health meal."

The "logic" underlying the health meal was that if individuals could not keep themselves, their clothes, or their rooms clean, they must be suffering from "an energy deficit" and that once the energy deficit was removed, the individual would regain the energy needed to keep himself, his clothing, and his room clean. The energy deficit would be removed by having a "health meal" rather than the usual meal served for dinner. The health meal involved eating as much high protein cereal as desired and having a vitamin pill. To those individuals who preferred eating the usually appetizing regular dinner to the cereal, the health meal was very effective in "restoring" the necessary energy to keep clean. The health meal is very effective when an individual comes down to dinner dirty and is given the meal. Usually one or two health meals is sufficient to remind the resident to wash up and to have clean clothes at dinner time.

The health meal is very effective for residents who cannot think of ways of getting around the health meal. Resourceful residents might eat out or wait until late evening and sneak food from the kitchen when no one is around. In general, however, the health meal is effective with many residents; it was, in addition, well-received and thought to be funny by the residents.

Although we have found the behavior modification approach to be very effective in altering the behaviors of our residents, one should not discount other approaches in helping residents. Residents who appear verbal, sensitive and insightful can and have achieved individual progress and growth from talking with the housemanagers and assistant housemanagers as one would approach family or friends for advice, guidance, or for seeking a different perspective on a particular problem.

We have successfully altered behavior by looking at behavior from a power-tactic point of view (Haley 1963).

One of the residents was the "run-away" champion at the state school where he lived for 20 years before being placed in our community home. One year he averaged over 80 run-aways from the state school. Whenever this individual was approached or admonished, or told something he didn't agree with, his usual response was to run away. Usually in the late afternoon of the same day he ran away, he would be very adept at going into a police station, identifying himself and where he was from, and getting a ride back to the institution in a police car just in time for dinner. When this individual arrived at the community home, this "lifestyle" seemed to persist. After a few attempts to approach the resident failed (since he would run away before we had a chance to talk to him), we came upon a new tactic. The moment we finished talking to him or telling him something about a misbehavior, we ordered him out of the house for two hours. In ways, we out-maneuvered his maneuver, by telling him to "run-away" before he ran-away on his own. The moment we started this new tactic, he stopped running away. He then became more pleasant and cooperative around the house. A few weeks later he decided, on his own, to go back to the state school. One speculation on why he left the community home was that he no longer had the status, which enhanced his self-esteem, of being the "run away" record holder in the house as he did at the state school. If we had more time to develop a different, more adaptive and appropriate behavior to be valued, he might have remained in the house. On the other hand, he recently applied to be taken back to the community home, since he no longer likes living at the state school.

The importance of individualized behavioral programs should be underscored. Behavioral goals should be explicit, the means of implementing these goals should be spelled out, and the effectiveness of these programs evaluated and revised periodically. In our program, individualized behavioral programs are evaluated on a monthly basis, at which time housemanagers review the current individualized behavioral programs with the psychological consultant. At these meetings, there are discussions about which individual programs seem effective and should therefore be retained, which are ineffective and therefore in need of modification, and which goals should be dropped since they have been reached or demonstrated by the resident.

The types of goals selected for the individualized behavioral program should be determined by the housemanagers, psychological consultant, and the resident. Usually, after a resident has been in a community home for a few weeks, the housemanagers can get a clear picture of the types of goals that should be set for each resident. These goals are usually brought up to the resident at the group house meetings, and some agreement is made upon the goals to work towards. At the group meeting, the housemanagers also find out from the resident the kinds of skills or behaviors that the resident would like to develop. Once there is agreement on such goals, the psychological consultant assists the housemanager and resident by giving various suggestions on the implementation of these goals.

Group House Meetings

In the community home program for adults, a house meeting is held each week in the early evening for a few hours. All individuals living in the house are expected to be at the meeting; this includes the residents, both housemanagers, and the assistant housemanager. The meeting usually is held following dinner and is held early enough not to interfere with the residents' plans for the later evening.

The meeting serves several important functions, with the function varying as different needs and problems arise. The length of the meeting also varies according to the topics and areas for consideration and discussion at the meeting.

One function of the meeting is to provide a setting in which the housemanagers can convey important information to the residents. The information might involve changes in application forms for benefits, vocational opportunities and information, changes in policy at Community Homes, new services, activities, and recreational opportunities available in the community.

The house meeting also provides opportunities for the staff to share their evaluation of a resident's progress and to compliment the residents on their progress. Sometimes five to ten minutes of a meeting consists of people complimenting each other for demonstrating new ways of acting or doing things. Here the staff are sometimes complimented by the residents for doing a fine job.

The house meeting also serves as a forum where residents and staff can bring up any problem that appears to be present in the house. People are encouraged to talk about the problems or bad feelings existing between themselves and other residents in the house. Often, once the conflict is openly expressed at the meeting, the problem can be quickly resolved, either through mutual agreements, role playing, compromises, or by solutions suggested by the housemanager. Expressing problems as they arise rather than waiting until the problems become explosions is a very helpful technique and often appreciated by the residents.

Besides using the meeting to voice complaints or problems, time is also spent giving the residents opportunities to make suggestions for changes and innovations in house procedures. Sometimes these suggestions are quite good. Meeting time is also used for planning house parties and activities that the entire house would find interesting.

Some of the outgrowths of this kind of house meeting are that it provides residents with opportunities to participate in a democratic group activity, to be respected and heard, and to have some opportunity to make responsible decisions that affect their own lives.

When we first held house meetings that emphasized the above mentioned areas, residents were very reluctant to acknowledge problems they were having in the house. Residents were also very obsequious, passive, and unsure about how they could participate at such a meeting. Years of institutionalization probably made a democratic meeting appear alien to them, and it also probably fostered a variation of the "don't rat on the other guy" set of values, which might have adaptive functions for surviving in an institutional setting. In time, however, residents began to see how discussing problems could lead to feeling better, about themselves and others, and that talking about feelings leads to the solution of problems rather than to restrictions or punishments. The meetings also gave residents opportunities to make suggestions that led to people acting upon their suggestions and demonstrated to residents that they could make valuable contributions to their own and other people's lives.

Workshops

In addition to the individualized behavioral programs, a different set of learning opportunities was considered important to develop further the skills that are necessary for independent living. Although considerable progress was being made by residents with the individualized programs, there were realistic limitations to the time and energy necessary for the housemanagers to foster the development of such skills. Some of our residents were going to evening school to get their high school diplomas, or equivalency diplomas, but the progress made at night school had more to do with academic rather than life skills. We were looking for a way to increase the residents' social, sexual, physical, and self-sufficiency skills. From this need, came the idea of the workshop.

Since there were four adult community homes in our program, we asked the housemanagers in the four homes whether they would be interested in conducting a workshop to develop additional skills for our residents in the above mentioned specialized areas. The housemanagers' responses were quite favorable, and the following week each housemanager couple came up with an area of interest and an outline of the specific topics to be covered in the specialized area. Information would be given to the residents in lecture form, with visual aids, and other methods of instruction would also be used, such as discussion, role playing, and other engaging ways in which people can be taught concepts.

The workshop was to last for eight weeks and include about eight people, preferably equally distributed from the four adult homes. Once there was agreement on the four topics for the workshops, each housemanager assigned their residents to the different workshops on the basis of which skills needed the most development. The housemanagers suggested that the workshop would be given the same night each week, last one hour for eight weeks, and that refreshments and a party-like atmosphere should follow the workshop.

After the first eight-week workshop ended, there would be an evaluation assessing the effectiveness of the workshop. If, indeed, the workshop seemed effective and was well-received by the residents, then it would continue with the selection of eight people from each house into a different workshop to be taught by a different set of housemanagers. In effect, there would be four workshops, with cycles of eight weeks each, and residents would have an opportunity to learn additional skills in four separate areas within a period of 32 weeks.

Families of the Residents

There is considerable variation in the way a resident's family reacts to the placement of the resident into a community home after the resident has been living at a state school. Some parents and siblings have always remained in touch with the resident while the resident was institutionalized and continue such visits after the resident moves into a community home. The contact between the resident and such families often consists of family visits to the community home, their taking the resident out for dinner, or their having the resident spend a weekend or time during holidays in their own homes. The families who have maintained contact with the resident usually are pleased that their sons or daughters are once again living in the community. Often these families are quite helpful in contributing time, old furniture, and just being generally helpful in different ways.

When the name and address of a resident's family is known, housemanagers assist and encourage the residents to re-establish or maintain contact with members of their families. Many times having the resident re-establish contact with his family proves rewarding both to the resident and to the family. Sometimes families can accept and be closer to the resident than they were when he was institutionalized. Residents probably have a great deal of feelings about why they were institutionalized, and providing new contact with the family gives the resident more opportunities to deal with these feelings. Just seeing what one's parents and family looks like twenty years later and having the family see the resident twenty years later can be very constructive, rewarding experiences.

Re-establishing contact with families for some of our residents is difficult. Some residents were placed in institutions when they were infants or toddlers. Many of the parents of these individuals have virtually abandoned them by never writing, visiting, or providing changes of address to the institution. To find these individual families would be a herculean task, and unfortunately there is not sufficient time nor personnel in our organization to track down the families of these residents.

A related situation exists for some of our residents who were placed into community homes when they were in their forties and fifties. Many of the parents of these individuals have passed away, although at times, we have achieved some success in getting in touch with a concerned sibling or uncle, or some member of the resident's extended family who remembers and still shows some concern for the resident.

Perhaps the most difficult situation involving a resident's family is when the family resists and rejects the idea of the resident's being discharged from the institution. Many of these families insist that the resident is incapable of functioning in the community. There can be many different reasons why families react this way. Seeing one's child successfully living in the community probably elicits guilt feelings in the families who originally institutionalized their child because they envisioned the child as never being able to function in the community. Seeing their child function successfully in the community might make these families feel that they made a grave mistake in having prematurely written off their child.

Other families may resist seeing and having the resident return to the community because institutionalizing such a child might serve a family function in maintaining a family homeostasis or balance in order to keep the family functioning (Jackson 1957). The prospect of having this "identified patient" or "problem" return to the community (and perhaps the fear of the resident eventually returning to the family) becomes a potential threat to the family balance that has been maintained while the resident was removed from the family.

Fortunately, families resistant to the idea of their child leaving the institution and returning to the community have very little recourse. Often when a child is placed in a state school for the retarded, the state school or the state becomes the legal guardian for that individual. Thus, when the state, as the legal guardian, decides that living in a community home is in the best interests of a particular individual, the resisting family of origin has few legal options. It is supposed that if these resisting parents did have legal recourse, there would be too much social pressure and embarrassment involved in parents bringing the state into legal proceedings in order to reinstitutionalize their child.

Families opposed to their children living in the community do express this resistance in more subtle ways. Sometimes the resistance takes the form of their continual expression of doubts, both to the community home staff and to the resident, that the resident can take care of himself and live in the community. Often these parents feel that the resident should receive closer supervision and not be placed in situations that might lead to failure, disappointment, or getting hurt.

Family resistance also can be inferred when a resident returns from a weekend visit to his family, and appears quite upset. These individuals might request the useless medication that they had been taking at the institution and that had been successfully reduced or eliminated once they came to live in the community home. Or, reminiscent of the institutional days, they might display bizarre behaviors that had also been eliminated within the first few weeks of living in the community home. It appears that home visits elicit regressive behaviors with some of our residents, and this regressive shift is probably an outgrowth of family resistance to accepting the resident living in the community, or "returning" home.

The regressive shift in behavior is usually temporary once the resident returns to the community home, and the amount of time necessary for the resident to begin acting more maturely varies on an individual basis. When home visits become very upsetting for residents or if the regressive behavior is maintained for more than a few weeks, we take more active steps in ensuring that these occurrences do not happen again.

First, we inform the family about the degree of disruption and regression that has taken place as a function of the resident's home visit. We then, with the approval of the resident, impose temporary limits on the procedures for home visits. Usually the limits take the form of restricting the resident from home visits for a month or so or until the resident no longer displays the regressive behavior. After the recovery period, we inform the resident and the family that they can see each other under certain conditions. These conditions consist of the family being invited to see the resident at the resident's community home. When a few of these visits appear to have been successful, then visits to the resident's family home can be resumed.

There are many advantages to having the family visit the resident at the community home. First, it reduces the possibility of the resident showing regressive behavior. Since the visiting family is on foreign ground and being scrutinized by the community home staff and other residents in the home, they are more likely to act like guests than like family. Thus, the resident being visited has the opportunity to enjoy their family without being subjected to some of the upsetting features that would occur in the family's home.

Another advantage of having the family visit the resident is to demonstrate to the resident that the family is interested in the resident and is willing to spend the time and energy involved in making a visit. The visit also enables the family to meet and spend some time with the housemanagers and other residents and perhaps obtain a more realistic picture of the community home.

In general, when residents become upset and begin showing regressive behaviors as a consequence of a visit with their families, limits are placed on both the resident and the family. The limits provide a "cooling-off" period for the resident and give the housemanagers sufficient time to plan programs that lead to teaching the resident and the resident's family how both can spend more time with each other in enjoyable rather than disruptive ways. The power to impose the above mentioned limits on both the resident and his family probably comes from the resident's enjoying living in the community home and not wishing to return to the institution. Limits can be placed on the resident's family probably because the family is not interested in seeing the resident return to the institution nor, unfortunately, are they interested in having the resident return to their own home.

We are presently experimenting in other ways with families who are resistant to the idea of their sons or daughters living in the community rather than in an institution. In Massachusetts, residents are placed in community homes that are in the same cachement areas where the residents were living before they were placed in institutions. There are, therefore, times when the resident is placed in a community home located in the same town where his family is presently living. This sometimes produces a "too close for comfort" situation both for the resident and the family, and we are presently exploring new approaches to these problems by, for example, inviting the family to the community home for conferences that include the housemanager, psychological consultant, and the resident. During these conferences we emphasize how the resident and his family can cooperate in the behavioral programs that the community home staff has developed to change the resident's behavior. These changes would eventually result in more rewarding experiences for both the resident and the family. Since we are just beginning to experiment with these conferences, it is too early to assess the effectiveness of this particular approach in assisting the resident or the resident's family.

Criteria for Placement into the Community

Our community home program for adults has had a rather *laissez-faire* and perhaps passive attitude about when a resident is ready to move into an independent living situation. Residents generally know that the community home can become their permanent residence if that is their choice. On the other hand, and we may be presenting residents with mixed messages, residents also know that the community home program is basically oriented to help residents develop the skills necessary to live independently in the community.

Usually the resident, rather than the housemanager, initially brings up the subject of moving out of the community home and into an apartment. When the housemanagers feel that the resident does have the necessary skills for independent living, the resident is encouraged to pursue this matter further with the assistance of the housemanagers. Further discussions between the resident and housemanager continue, and the resident is assisted in as many ways as possible in making the move from the community home to an independent living situation.

The situation becomes more complicated and difficult when a resident expresses interest in moving into an apartment and the housemanagers do not feel that the necessary skills for independent living have been developed. In such situations, the resident is discouraged from making the move until the necessary undeveloped skills are developed. Usually verbal discouragement expressed by the housemanagers suffices in keeping the resident in the community home program. The housemanagers and the resident then decide on the deficiencies that exist, and a program is devised to accelerate the development of these skills.

The criteria used by housemanagers in judging when a resident is ready for independent living are based upon the resident's vocational, social, and self-sufficiency skills. Since a resident must be employed in a sheltered workshop or in a competitive employment setting in order to live in a community home, by the time a resident leaves the community home, he or she has already displayed satisfactory vocational adjustment and skills for about one to one and a half years.

Similarly, living in a community home, with an effective behavioral program, usually leads to the elimination of most bizarre behaviors, and the development of the social skills necessary to function in an independent living situation. Naturally, the community home staff would like to go beyond the development of functional social skills "for getting by" and develop social skills that would lead to more meaningful, rich, and socially rewarding lives. This hope might indeed be too idealistic and should be kept in perspective by observing the level of social skills developed in the general population already living in the community.

Assessing self-sufficiency skills can readily be determined by the housemanagers who, after being in the same house with the resident for a year or so, have a fairly realistic picture of how well the resident can take care of himself. If certain self-sufficiency skills have not been developed, or should be further developed, then these skills are placed on the behavioral chart and become an important part of the resident's individualized behavioral program.

Follow-up Procedures for Ex-Residents

When a resident leaves the community home for a more independent living situation, there are several ways in which we maintain contact with the resident to insure that the resident is getting along and that things are going well. The effectiveness of these follow-up procedures varies with the particular resident.

Before the resident departs from the community home, we invite the resident to continue attending the weekly meetings and to join the residents in the community home for dinner preceding the meeting. By attending the weekly meetings, the ex-resident has an opportunity to maintain ties and emotional support from the housemanagers and some friends living in the community home. Residents also are informed that they are more than welcome to drop in and have dinner at their old home whenever they please.

Another opportunity to follow-up the ex-resident occurs when the ex-resident remains working in the sheltered workshop and thus maintains contact with staff members who are associated with both the workshop and the community home program. Some of the support and counseling available in the sheltered workshop setting can easily be applied to problems and difficulties that the ex-resident might be having in his new residence.

A third follow-up procedure involves the use of a community-oriented team of professionals who provide services to retarded individuals living in institutions and in the community. In Massachusetts, the team is organized and funded by the Department of Mental Health, and is known as DART (Diagnostic Assessment and Reevaluation Team). The two basic functions of the team are to provide case-management services and to assess the needs of retarded people on a regional basis. Case-management involves assisting the ex-resident by providing information about vocational, social, financial, recreational, and health matters and by being available and of general assistance to the ex-resident in his adjustment to independent living.

When a resident is about to leave the community home, the DART team is contacted and given the name, address, and any other relevant information about the resident. The team then initiates contact and follow-up procedures with the ex-resident. The team also continues to inform the community home program about the ex-resident's progress.

Hopefully, the idea of case-management and follow-up teams are well developed and implemented in many states. Such teams are vital in insuring the effectiveness of any community home program. Such teams, whether under a different name or funded by different state organizations, should be contacted a few months before any community home resident is placed into an independent living situation. If such teams do not exist, then the necessary lobbying (see Chapter 4) should begin immediately after a home is established in order to have such a team available when residents begin to leave the community home.

There is a fourth follow-up procedure that is useful but also probably peculiar to small towns (20 to 30,000 population) such as those in which our six community homes have been established. Many of the community home residents and staff "bump into" ex-residents in town in the course of daily routines, and from the ordinary "chit-chat" that goes on during these brief encounters, considerable information is exchanged. This information is then placed into a definite yet incomprehensible grapevine that yields fairly accurate information in short periods of time. Sometimes within a few hours, housemanagers, the director, and sometimes the psychological consultant who is relatively removed from the homes, learn through this grapevine about ex-residents being hired or fired from jobs, breaking a leg, getting engaged, and so forth. The grapevine does provide some information about ex-residents and is an interesting phenomenon in that it carries the juicier and more interesting aspects of human affairs. Information from the grapevine should, however, be viewed with the usual skepticism, and should be no replacement for a formal, organized, complete follow-up procedure.

There are certain problems with following-up ex-residents that will occur independently of the follow-up services available. What does one do when an ex-resident wants to have nothing to do with any person or agency who wishes to be helpful or to be of assistance to him?

One of our residents lived in a community home for over a year and displayed a considerable degree of independence and self-sufficiency skills at the time he entered the community home. During his tenure in the home, it was virtually impossible to make suggestions, directives, or get close to him in any way. Although rebellious with respect to being receptive to anything suggested by the housemanager or consultant, he nevertheless was responsible, did his jobs, and fulfilled the basic prerequisites for living in the community home. He was resistive to any attempt to change him through our behavioral programs to the point where the housemanagers gave up trying to be helpful or receptive. Although he changed considerably during the year that he was in the home, the changes are attributed to the ambience and permissiveness of the home and not to any form of direct intervention such as a behavioral program. One day, he threatened to leave the home, and the housemanagers, knowing he had the necessary skills to live outside of a community home, called his bluff and encouraged the move. He then moved out of the community home and has been living for two years by himself in the community and is doing quite well. He receives constant invitations to dinners, parties, picnics, and other activities from residents, housemanagers, and other community home staff, but rejects them all, although now he rejects such offers politely. It seems as though he wants to completely disassociate himself from anything and anyone related to institutions, retardation, community homes or even concerned individuals.

How does one follow-up such an individual? How many of our concerns are realistic, and how much of our concern smacks of an over-involved parent?

Where does one draw the line between being available and caring and intruding on an individual's right for privacy and to be left alone? How much of our concern becomes worrying over the resident's risk-taking and failures, which are necessary for the ex-resident to further develop his confidence and to become more self-sufficient?

There are, of course, no simple answers to these questions. One answer to some of these questions will come from our own and other research programs. Continuous monitoring of ex-residents, with one-, two-, five-, and possibly ten-year follow-up evaluations will begin to give us some information about whether the concerns about the welfare of the ex-resident are realistic.

Research Findings

In January 1974 a formal research program was initiated to evaluate the effectiveness of the community home program on the behavior of our residents. The *Adaptive Behavioral Scale* was completed by our housemanagers for all of the residents living in the adult and children homes. These *ABS* scores have been reported earlier in this chapter. In January 1975 the same test scores will be obtained to see if differences in scores and behavior have occurred within this one-year period. Scores obtained on our residents will also be compared with scores obtained from matched control subjects who are living in a state school for the retarded. This is the same state school where our present community homes residents formerly lived. The results of this particular research project will be published at a later date. Table 7–7 provides some information on the progress made by the first eleven residents referred from a state school to the Crescent Street house within a two-and-one-half-year period. The data presented in Table 7–7 are impressive, from our point of view, with two residents returning to the state school, five residents successfully living independently in the community, and four residents remaining in the community home. The five ex-residents presently living in the community are all working in a competitive or sheltered work situation, appear happy and healthy, and are seen actively involved in community recreations (as reported by the aforementioned grapevine).

The success story of some of the Crescent Street residents must be viewed with some qualifications. First, we are viewing a community home program that involves very small numbers of people who are being considered within a short (two and a half years) period of time. It would be fruitful to have a larger number of residents viewed within longer periods of time to answer some crucial questions: what is the average or necessary time for a resident to be in a community home program in order to develop the necessary

Table 7-7
Progress and Current Status of Crescent Street Residents [a]

Resident	Age	Duration in Community Home	Present Living Situation	Duration in New Living Situation	Vocational Status
A	32	6 Days	State School		
B	48	2 Months	State School		
C	50	9 Months	Apartment/Self	24 Months	Competitive Employment
D	28	15 Months	Apartment/Self	19 Months	Competitive Employment
E	41	17 Months	Apartment/Married	16 Months	Sheltered Workshop
F	40	26 Months	Apartment/Roommate	3 Months	Competitive Employment
G	31	12 Months	Apartment/Roommate	3 Months	Competitive Employment
H	51	25 Months	Community Home		Sheltered Workshop
I	22	34 Months	Community Home		Sheltered Workshop
J	50	14 Months	Community Home		Sheltered Workshop
K	23	10 Months	Community Home		Sheltered Workshop

[a] Formerly living at state school.

skills to live independently in the community? What are the characteristics of people who can and cannot adjust to a community home situation? How well will the five ex-residents presently living in the community do five or ten years from now? Unfortunately, the answers to these questions are not presently available but hopefully will be available as more research is performed on community home programs.

The second qualification to consider when looking at the Crescent Street information is the characteristics of the residents who were placed into this community home. Since Crescent Street was one of the first community homes developed in Region I, in Massachusetts, the residents referred by the state school were functioning at more developed levels than the residents who are presently being referred. Comparing the *ABS* scores of the present residents at Crescent Street with the residents in the other houses (see Table 7–5) supports the view that the former display more developed skills and consequently were more easily placed into independent living situations in a relatively short period of time. We anticipate that the residents in some of the other homes, who have less-developed skills, will probably remain in community homes for longer periods of time before they are placed successfully into independent living situations.

There are less data available on the three other adult homes since these homes have been in existence for only eight months. There are, however, some preliminary findings that can be reported. Scores from the *ABS* for the residents in these homes are reported in Tables 7–2, 7–3, and 7–4.

Of the 27 residents placed into the three community homes, three have returned to the state school by their own request. Of these, two male residents returned to the state school after living in a community home less than a week. The third resident lived in a community home for two months and returned to the state school because she could not have her own way with the housemanagers and because she would not abide by the house procedures. All of the remaining 24 residents, with the exception of one, are working in a sheltered workshop or are involved in a day activity program run by the workshop. The one exception is presently working in a competitive employment setting, and we're all very proud of him.

References

Adaptive Behavior Scale. 1974. Washington, D.C.: American Association on Mental Deficiency.

Haley, J. 1963. *Strategies of Psychotherapy.* New York: Grune and Stratton.

Jackson, D. D. 1957. "The Question of Family Homeostasis." *Psychiatric Quarterly Supplement* 31:79–90.

Keller, O. J. and B. S. Alper. 1970. *Halfway Houses: Community-Centered Correction and Treatment.* Lexington, Mass.: Lexington Books, D. C. Heath.

Premack, D. 1959. "Towards Empirical Behavioral Laws. I. Positive Reinforcement." *Psychological Review* 66:219–33.

Reppucci, N. D. and J. T. Saunders. 1974. "Social Psychology of Behavior Modification: Problems of Implementation in Natural Settings." *American Psychologist* 29:649–60.

Thompson, T. and J. Grabowski, eds. 1972. *Behavior Modification of the Mentally Retarded.* New York: Oxford University Press.

Webster, D. R. and N. H. Azrin. 1973. "Required Relaxation: A Method of Inhibiting Agitative-Disruptive Behavior of Retardates." *Behavior Research and Therapy* 11:67–78.

Appendixes

Appendix A:
Housemanager's Job
Description

There are basically five areas of responsibility that comprise the job of housemanager. These are as follows:

1. The housemanagers are responsible for the physical operation of the community residence, in the areas of food procurement and preparation, housekeeping, maintenance, and utility upkeep.

2. The housemanagers are responsible for the daily affairs and welfare of the residents living with them. This includes the areas of nutrition, dress, sleep, medical services, dental services, and special services. Further that the housemanagers oversee the residents use of money. Finally, that the housemanagers are responsible for making sure that the residents are involved in an appropriate day activity and recreational program suited to their needs and abilities.

3. The housemanagers are responsible for the creation and implementation of suitable behavioral programs and in-house training programs to provide the resident with the skills and behaviors necessary to live comfortably and responsibly within the community residence, and the larger community.

4. The housemanagers are responsible for creating and maintaining communication and liaisons with the appropriate personnel in various state and private agencies so that residents may fully utilize the services and opportunities these agencies provide.

5. The housemanagers are responsible for the hiring, training, supervision and evaluation of their staff.

Appendix B:
Behavioral Chart

FULL NAME _____ MONTH _____ YEAR _____ NAME OF INDIVIDUAL COMPLETING FORM _____

Description of Current Behavior in Specific Terms (Examples of Actual Behavior)	Alternative Behaviors to Replace Behaviors to be Weakened	Method of Modifying Behavior	MONTH 1 2 3 4 5	MONTH 1 2 3 4 5

Appendix C:
House Selection Guide Form

Street: _____, Town: _____, Zoning: _____
Street number: _____   Present Owner: _____
                                 Address: _____

Location.

Near: _____   _____

_____   _____

Far From: _____

Lot Size: _____
Lot Characteristics: _____

_____

Outside of House.

Condition: _____

Windows: _____

Roof: _____

Comments: _____

_____

_____

Inside of House.

Rooms. Number: _____
Bedrooms. Number: _____
    Size: _____, Cap: _____   Size: _____, Capacity: _____
    Size: _____, Cap: _____   Size: _____, Capacity: _____
    Size: _____, Cap: _____   Size: _____, Capacity: _____
    Comments: _____

Kitchen. Size: _____, Utilities: _____

Comments: _____

_____

Bathrooms. Number: _____, Size: _____
    Comments: _____
_____

Cellar. Size: _____, Condition: _____
_____
    Comments: _____
_____

Utilities.

Electrical: _____
Plumbing: _____
Heating: _____
Gas: _____
Comments: _____
_____

Appendix D: Sample Budget for A Community Residence for Adults (Annual)

Salaries:
    Housemanger Couple:.................... $11,500
    Relief Manager.......................... 6,000
    Director.............................. 4,000
                                                       $21,500
Fringe Benefits (15%)................................ 3,225
General and Administrative........................... 3,000
Consulting.. 3,000
                                                         $30,725
Transportation...................................... 1,500
Telephone... 350
Utilities... 2,100
Rental.. 4,800
Food.. 6,760
Maintenance... 1,000
Insurance... 300
Miscellaneous expenses.............................. 500
                                                         $17,310
      Total................................
                                                         $48,035

Appendix E: Sample Budget for a Community Residence for Children (Annual)

Salaries:

Housemanager couple	$12,000		
Relief Managers (3)	15,300		
Director	4,000		
		$31,300	
Fringe Benefits (15%)		4,695	
General and Administrative		2,500	
Consulting		5,000	$43,495
Transportation		2,000	
Telephone		500	
Utilities		2,500	
Rent		7,200	
Food		6,000	
Maintenance		1,000	
Insurance		300	
			$19,500
Total			$62,995

Index

Index

About the Editor and Contributors

Joel S. Bergman is an assistant professor of psychology at Smith College, a behavioral program consultant to the Community Homes Program, and a consultant in behavior modification to the Hospital Improvement Program at the Northampton (Mass.) State Hospital. Since September 1970 he and the students in his courses have been working with institutionalized populations of disturbed and retarded people in an effort to place them into the community. The author of several articles in *Psychophysiology* and the *American Journal of Orthopsychiatry,* Dr. Bergman received the Ph.D. in clinical psychology from Bowling Green State University.

Joan C. Cronin is a community liaison person with the Mental Retardation Representation Project in Northampton, Massachusetts, a legal services project established to define and disseminate information and interpretation of laws governing the legal and civil rights of retarded citizens leaving institutions. The parent of a retarded child, Ms. Cronin has been active in the Hampshire County Association for Retarded Citizens and is a former president of that organization. She is also vice-president of the Franklin/Hampshire Area Mental Health Board, chairman of the Mental Retardation Subcommittee, and a member of the Regional Mental Health Advisory Council and the Regional Mental Retardation Advisory Council.

William P. Gerry is a graduate of the University of Massachusetts at Amherst. He and his wife opened the Crescent Street community residence discussed in this book. Since 1972, he has been involved in setting up and directing three additional community residences.

Margaret Tomasko Gerry received her education at Smith College and the University of Massachusetts at Amherst. Aside from her involvement with the community residence, she is director of Community Homes for Children, Inc.